Praise for *Scarlet Macaw Ascending*

"Dr. Sarah's debut memoir is beautifully written & profound. Her book is a testament & living documentation of the transformative power of recognizing burnout, as well as the potency of the medicines of skilled support, community, rest, & immersive healing experiences. Sarah writes with exceptional wisdom & sensitivity about the complex layers of burnout, nervous system dysregulation, & trauma that so many of us veterinarians carry. Her narrative is deeply personal & vulnerable, offering hope & healing to others who may see themselves in her story of self-betrayal, severe burnout, exhaustion, & ultimately the courage to take a leap of faith towards healing. I truly was so moved I could not put this book down."

—**Eve Harrison**, VMD, CVA, CVPM, CCFP, The House Call Vet Academy (Continuing Education & Community)

"*Scarlet Macaw Ascending* is a brutally honest account of Dr. Sarah's raw pain, as she journeys towards healing and wholeness. A page turning story that pulls you in and doesn't let you go even after you've read the last word."

—**Carolyne Cook**, MSN, APRN-C

"This book is an inspiration to us all. Sarah takes us on a journey from dealing with the challenges life throws at us to finding balance and harmony. If you have ever struggled with your life being out of balance this story will guide you to the path of reconnecting with the resources that will reset your life. A must read in today's world where life can seem out of control."

—**Mike Art**, LCSW

"Costa Rica and its people, animals, and natural beauty are magical. Sarah transported me so effectively with her sensory experiences of the place that I could genuinely envision, smell, feel what it is like to be in this sanctuary of peace and healing. Having a sense of the entirety of the experience is what moves the reader so deeply as Sarah poetically and vulnerably weaves her story of past and present as she shares her memories of the December veterinary wellness retreat at Wild Sun Wildlife Sanctuary.

"Her reflections, moments of growth, and rekindling of lifeforce energy and purpose touch our collective human hearts, particularly those of us that can identify with experiencing burnout as professional caregivers. Thank you for sharing this spiritual awakening with us. I feel fortunate to have been alongside you then and now."

—**Sonja A. Olson**, DVM, C-MMT, Veterinary Health & Wellness Educator, Founder: Heartstorming Wellness, Author of *Creating Well-being and Building Resilience in the Veterinary Profession: A Call to Life*

Scarlet Macaw Ascending

A Memoir

Sarah Burkindine

ISBN: 979-8-9931936-0-1 (Paperback)
979-8-9931936-1-8 (Hardcover)
979-8-9931936-2-5 (eBook)

CONTENTS

INTRODUCTION

WHEN SURVIVAL BECOMES NORMAL, it's almost impossible to recognize how deeply you're suffering. I spent years living in survival mode and had forgotten how to relax and enjoy my life. Exhaustion and stress were familiar—like old, trusted friends. So, I didn't hear my body's quiet pleas for rest.

If someone had pointed out that this pace was unsustainable, I don't know if I would have listened. From the outside, I was living the American Dream. But sometimes the truth can only be seen when we're finally ready.

That day came when I learned about a veterinary wellness retreat and seminar on burnout in Costa Rica. It wasn't a vacation—it was a rehabilitation.

Originally, I began journaling to record, in vivid detail, the entirety of my trip. I didn't want to forget a thing. This experience had become sacred: a quiet, profound transformation. As I wrote, I realized that my story was not just for me. Others shared pieces of their journeys that sounded like echoes of mine.

It became clear: maybe my story could matter.

Maybe it could be the wake-up call that someone else needs—the gentle nudge toward seeking help sooner than I did.

My goal is not to preach or to present myself as an expert. I am simply someone who lived it. This book is one person's honest journey through burnout and recovery. I share the vulnerable moments, the small triumphs, and the unexpected rediscovery of self, hoping to start a bigger conversation about healing, sustainable living, and how we reclaim ourselves.

In these pages, you can expect moments of rawness, painful reckonings, and glimpses of hope. It is not a perfect story—but it is a real one. It is mine.

Without realizing it, I had been quietly dismantling old, maladaptive narratives for years. My time in Costa Rica simply sped up the process.

This is the story of how I found the courage to breathe fully into myself—and create my new story. I invite you to walk with me through the heartache, the wonder, the letting go, and the coming home.

Welcome

CHAPTER 1

Scarlet Macaw Ascending

SCARLET MACAWS ARE SPECTACULARLY beautiful as they fly in formation, screaming out to each other—*RAAAAAAK!*—like war cries echoing throughout the jungle. Like watching the perfect maneuvers and symmetry of the Navy's Blue Angels, they soar brilliantly through the sky. Their plumage is a feast for the eyes, beginning with deep scarlet red, followed by sunlit yellow and royal blue. Scarlet tail feathers drape over the blue, allowing the brilliance beneath to peek through.

I had come to Costa Rica for healing, burnt out from years of caregiving and self-neglect. Sleepless nights and silent resentment—my norm—though I'd only recently admitted it to myself. But there was something about watching these macaws—how they thrived in community, how they screamed, unapologetically loudly—that cracked something open in me emotionally. I saw in them what I had long forgotten in myself: boldness, instinct, and color.

Curious and captivated by the macaws, I began to learn more about them. Found primarily in the rainforests of Central and South America, scarlet macaws live as bonded pairs in flocks of thirty or so, called a pandemonium, separating only when the female is nesting, and the male goes out to find food. They eat mainly fruits and nuts, often eating the fruit before it is ripe—something other birds cannot do—giving them an advantage. They also ingest clay from riverbeds to help protect them against toxins found in their food. This clay helps neutralize the toxins that they cannot avoid in their search for nourishment. These adaptations enabled their survival allowing them to flourish where others cannot. I, like the macaws, hoped to find my own clay to help protect me from the things that used to nourish me—my passion, my profession, my calling to be a caretaker for others—that had turned to poison within me. Watching them adapt so elegantly to a toxic environment made me realize how clumsily I had been trying to do the same thing.

Despite such protections and advantages, these majestic parrots have seen their numbers plummet throughout Costa Rica. Between the 1940's and 1990's, around half of the population was lost. Deforestation from human activity as well as illegal trade were the main causes of the decline. The chicks were taken and could be sold or traded, particularly to Americans, where they could fetch $300-400. The adults could bring closer to $2000-4000. In Costa Rica alone, where these birds used to inhabit up to 85% of the country, now they are found in only a few isolated areas. Learning that these gorgeous parrots had been lost to so much of the world left me grief-stricken—much like hearing of lives lost in an earthquake, overwhelming in scope and sorrow. I, too, was living in the aftermath of seismic shock waves in my own life.

Conservation and breeding programs have sparked hope, with populations climbing nearly 50% in recent years. Many of these rehabilitation facilities have been able to confiscate stolen birds who have been domesticated and use them for their breeding programs, allowing their chicks to re-enter the wild. They have created nesting boxes, a safe space for pairs to hide from predators. Trees have been planted to increase access to food. In addition to plans made to help the birds, educational programs have been launched to inform surrounding communities, including school-aged children, of the dangers of illegal trade and deforestation. If not stopped, the scarlet macaws could head towards extinction.

During a week in Costa Rica, I watched them soar through the skies calling out to one another from across the jungle. I couldn't help but think what a shame it would be to never be able to see these dazzling creatures of flight. I also reflected on the similarities between Wild Sun Rescue—the scarlet macaw rehab facility where I stayed—and Pura Vida Wellness Retreats, the source of my own healing in Costa Rica. Both provided care and restoration—for the macaws and for me, ensuring our survival.

CHAPTER 2

The Brink of Extinction

I WENT TO COSTA Rica to learn about burnout and how to heal from it. It became clear—I had been living in survival mode. I was robotic in going from task to task, stopping only for sleep—which wasn't even restful. It was fragmented, never restorative. I had convinced myself that chores around the house were hobbies so that I could fool myself into thinking that I wasn't working nonstop. I told myself that my children and work came above all else. Rest came only when neither the kids nor work needed me—stopping before then felt selfish. Without intervention, I was at a point where I could not survive any longer. I was on the brink of becoming extinct myself.

CHAPTER 3

The Downward Spiral

I HAD WANTED TO be a veterinarian for as long as I could remember. I have always loved animals. Though raised in a suburban part of Kansas City and only exposed to dogs, rabbits and one guinea pig growing up, I loved all animals. I loved getting to see the different animals from all over the world at our zoo. I used to spend hours studying the encyclopedia, poring over pictures of all the dog breeds listed under the label 'Dog'. I still have most of the images emblazoned in my memory despite never seeing many of the breeds in real life. Watching a horse run could elicit tears just from witnessing the sheer beauty of the animal and hearing the pounding of its hooves on the dirt below.

Getting accepted into vet school is still one of my crowning achievements, and I did not take my acceptance lightly, knowing that so many others did not get the same opportunity.

Vet school was a hard four years full of long days that rolled into long nights. Often, I studied into the wee hours of the morning, only getting a few hours of sleep before starting the same thing all over again the next day. With the rest of my class of one hundred similarly minded people, we created a community where we wanted to see each other succeed and help each other when it was needed. Shared adversity bonding is the creation of strong bonds with others who are working through difficult or challenging experiences together. Though I did not know this term back then, it explained how quickly we all became a family of sorts. Our first year, during an Intro to Veterinary Medicine course, one of the professors told us to look to our left and then to our right. Then, he announced that there was a good chance one of those people might not make it to the end of the four years. Rather than creating a competitive situation, it strengthened our class as we worked to ensure that everyone made it through together. We sat in lectures together, worked through lab classes together, studied together and helped each other through all the personal and academic issues that arose. Those four years spent in vet school were harder than the previous years of undergraduate coursework. We celebrated when someone's wife had a baby, and offered words of support when someone's marriage dissolved. We sat in silent togetherness when we learned about a classmate's flunking out and laughed together over a shared warped sense of humor when we were feeling overwhelmed. There is no way to explain what those four years meant to me and how grateful I am for getting to go through that part of my education with my classmates. The day after graduation, I sat on my couch in the living room crying over having to leave my school family. I was also terrified because I did not feel like I knew enough to be able to go out into the world and practice medicine, let alone without the rest of my class for support. While moving to Atlanta for a small animal and surgical internship instead of going directly into practice, I still needed to be competent—but that feeling eluded me.

My internship was a smaller version of vet school. Five other interns and I worked up to sixty to eighty hours per week learning from specialists throughout every facet of veterinary medicine. Once again, the six of us bonded over shared exhaustion, anxiety, educational growth, and experiences. We learned to push ourselves through the exhaustion that comes from working overnight ER shifts from five at night until nine the next morning. We learned to listen to everyone because learning also came from the technicians and front desk staff too. They had more experience than we did and taught us things beyond the vet school curriculum—like communicating with emotional clients, triaging emergencies, and practical tips that made patient care easier. Each day was already immensely stressful, but my relentless and harshly critical internal voice kept telling me that I was not smart enough to be there.

Even after twenty-three years, I still struggled with imposter syndrome—a persistent sense of self-doubt, inadequacy, and fear of being exposed as a fraud despite my achievements. In rare moments, I relaxed into my success as a veterinarian and allowed myself to believe that I was a knowledgeable professional. However, all of that dissipates the moment that someone else is upset with me. I delve into a downward spiral of shame, self-blame, and self-doubt. Striving for perfection seemed to be the only way to avoid the negative self-talk and anger from others. It worked too. The harder I worked and the more I did for my clients, the more positively those around me responded. I believed I could outrun imposter syndrome by doing just this, never thinking that this might be maladaptive or that I would eventually run myself into the ground.

Over the past twenty-three years of outpacing imposter syndrome, I've experienced major milestones and challenges as well. I got married, divorced and remarried. I had three wonderful children, all of whom are neurodivergent, and fought to get IEPs for two of them. I worked in two different veterinary clinics before leaving the second clinic to start my own mobile veterinary clinic.

Along the way, I navigated tough periods in my marriage, shaped by life's challenges and everything in between. What I failed to do was to take care of myself. I was so wrapped up in taking care of others. I tried so desperately to control my world, to avoid its inevitable collapse if I failed at anything, that I overlooked taking care of the one person who needed my attention the most.

Me.

I felt like a circus performer frantically keeping plates spinning on poles to prevent them from crashing. Each day, I went from one to another, caring for everyone in front of me, not realizing that I could not keep this pace going. I didn't know it yet, but something was about to shift. The smallest of signs—a Facebook ad, a whisper of curiosity—would begin to pull me towards salvation.

CHAPTER 4

The Seed of Recognition

OVER LABOR DAY WEEKEND last year, my daughter was performing in an Irish feis, a Gaelic word referring to an Irish dance competition. I booked a hotel for two nights to avoid getting up before sunrise to get ready and drive the thirty-five minutes downtown both days. Exhausted, I resented the early mornings more than ever. The idea of giving up most of my weekend to wake up even earlier than I do for work—just to spend the day in a crowded, noisy hotel ballroom full of anxious dancers and stressed-out parents—felt crushing.

As my husband drove our stuffed car downtown, I absently scrolled through Facebook. I saw an ad for a veterinary retreat in Alaska in January. Having no desire to set foot in Alaska during one of the coldest months, I was intrigued by the thought of a veterinary retreat. I had no concept of what this was, nor how it worked. I read the itinerary and some comments from people who had previously attended. There were seminars for continuing education aimed at teaching veterinarians how to manage their own mental and emotional wellbeing as well as time for fun experiences. My interest was piqued, and I could justify the cost of a wellness retreat because I would simultaneously get continuing education credits. Therefore, a wellness retreat felt worthwhile for the credits I would earn rather than for its actual wellness benefits. However, the idea of traveling to Alaska during the winter was not appealing to me. Now that I knew these retreats existed, I spent the rest of the drive downtown and a decent portion of that night researching veterinary wellness retreats in other locales. Unfortunately, there were none in the continental United States. The few that I found were in exotic places like Mexico, Fiji and Costa Rica. I had started to give up on the thought of going to a wellness retreat because I did not feel like I could justify the cost of the retreat plus airfare.

Instead, I had started looking for non-veterinary specific wellness retreats near me. There were a few in Kansas and several in Arkansas that looked interesting, but they were just two- or three-day retreats. They were all mostly geared towards meditation and yoga. I had almost given up on the idea of doing a retreat altogether, but there was something that kept nagging at me. One of the veterinary retreats was aimed at those who were experiencing burnout.

Until I started Googling it, I had no real understanding of burnout in the clinical sense. With each article, the truth sank in—I was already there. And with that recognition came a rising tide of shame and fear. They say awareness is the first step to healing, but I found only paralysis in it. Knowing I was drowning didn't mean I knew how to swim. I began scanning my life through a magnifying glass, zeroing in on every flaw—every missed moment as a mother, every doubt in my medical ability. The self-blame was relentless. When I realized that, without some intervention or treatment, I was destined to continue this existence indefinitely. Shame and terror had already taken root—and they were growing.

By late September, I knew that I needed help. I simply could not keep going by myself. I remembered something I'd once read about the difference between the horse and the mule. Horses will keep pushing themselves until they collapse whereas a mule will stop before that, knowing that it needs to rest. Nothing you can do will force the mule to keep going past its setpoint. I've always thought of myself more like the horse than the mule, and it has been a matter of pride for me. Being the horse, however, was how I had gotten to this point. I'd passed the point of exhaustion, and I was shutting down or collapsing.

So, I started looking up veterinary retreats again and kept coming back to Pura Vida Veterinary Retreats in Costa Rica. I emailed the owner with questions about the retreat, admitting to the fact that I was nervous about committing to this retreat, and that I was likely in burnout and survival mode. As I typed, the tears came pouring out, streaming down my cheeks. There is something so powerful about admitting this to someone else, about being so vulnerable, not to a total stranger, but to myself. Galina, the retreat owner and I spent several days emailing back and forth before I decided to take the first step towards treatment. Knowing that I couldn't go by myself, I told her to book a room for me and my husband. Then, I immediately called him, tears still pushing over the lower lids.

"Hello," said Sam.

"Hey," my voice betraying the fear and stress within me, "do you remember me telling you about the veterinary wellness retreats I was researching?" I asked.

"Yeah, what about them?" he asked.

This is where the full-blown crying started. "I think I need to do this," I said, my voice cracking between sobs as I sat in the sun on the deck, listening to the windchimes stir in the warm breeze.

"I think you do too," he replied.

"I tentatively put a hold on a room for two people in Costa Rica. But, looking at airfare, I can book a flight on Southwest from KCI to San Jose, Costa Rica, but I must find another flight from San Jose to Cabuya," I told him as I spoke while crying. "And I don't think I can do this by myself. I am nervous about traveling to a foreign country I've never been to. I know things haven't been great between us lately, but I need you to help me do this. You're the only one I can ask. I don't have anyone else who would go with me." We'd become more like roommates than spouses over the last eight or ten years. It felt like I'd been in mourning, grieving the loss of the person I married long ago. There was a time when I wouldn't have had to ask—when he would've noticed I was drowning before I did.

"Of course I will go with you," his voice softened—just a little—but I clung to that shift like it meant something. "I can go and lie on the beach and relax."

"First, this is in the jungle. I don't think it's near a beach, but there is a pool. So, you could go sit by the pool. And I'm going there for a reason. This isn't a vacation for me. So, I need you to know that," I said, a little annoyed that he was so excited and obviously not understanding the gravitas of the situation.

"I know. I'd be happy just to get away. I don't need to be entertained. I can just do my own thing," he said.

As the realization hit me that I was losing reasons not to go, the panic crept up again, slowly tightening its grip. I hung up with Sam and booked the Southwest flight to San Jose for both of us. As it turned out, it was much more difficult to figure out the booking for the flight from San Jose to Cabuya. After an hour of texting back and forth with Costa Rican Green Airways, I finally had our flights completely booked. Instead of the excitement that normally came whenever I had a vacation planned, the rush of remorse flooded me.

I was suddenly worried about the cost of this trip, the time away from work and the kids, and the fear of the unknown.

I tried to push away any and all thoughts about this trip for as long as I could. It was two and a half months away, after all. I continued to work and focus on surviving each day, forgetting altogether about this trip until I got an email asking for payment. For a day or so, the panic set in again, but was easily kicked down the road to be dealt with in the future. As the date approached, anxiety curled in my belly and climbed toward my chest. A black cloud hovered.

Then came the absurd thought—what if the retreat was a scam? I searched frantically online, looking for proof I wasn't about to get duped in some elaborate scheme. By nightfall, my nerves had unraveled completely. I pictured a *Romancing the Stone* scenario: jungle crashes, machetes, drug lords. Hilarious in hindsight. Terrifying, in the moment.

CHAPTER 5

The Weight of Goodbye

BY SATURDAY NIGHT, JUST hours before we were set to leave for the airport, I dropped the kids off at my parents' house. I stayed for dinner, though I had no appetite, pushing food around my plate to appear okay for their sake. My youngest, overwhelmed by our leaving, gave up on her meal and curled into my lap, her small body folding into mine, heaving with quiet sobs. I hadn't been apart from them in ages, and the pain of watching their sadness was matched only by the ache of my own. I told Sam that if I could have cancelled without losing my money, I would have cancelled right then and there. I was absolutely dreading my decision to go to Costa Rica. Since becoming a mother, I haven't wanted to travel without my kids at all. It had been nine years since I had left them and Scarlett, our youngest, hadn't even been born at that point.

I was hoping that this would be the hardest part of leaving, that waking up the next morning would be a little easier, but I was wrong.

CHAPTER 6

Holding My Broken Heart

I AWOKE THE NEXT morning at 2am with a feeling of dread at having to get out of my warm little cocoon. I was safe here, in bed, in my home. When I was here, especially with my children, I felt protected. I could insulate myself against whatever judgements, criticisms and negative emotions lay outside my front door, not knowing yet that there was another way to protect myself.

I dragged my body out of bed and to the bathroom feeling the cold hard tiles under my feet as I plodded. Since I'm not a huge coffee fan, I decided I needed some sort of caffeinated beverage as fuel. So, I went out and got two cans of Dr Pepper Zero and poured them into my thermos that I was going to be taking with me.

I trudged back to the bathroom and started taking my morning pills and brushing my teeth. Nervousness washed over me and hit my stomach as it then radiated down my limbs.

As I dried my hair, I glanced over to the tiny cheap heart pendant on its chain that my daughters had picked out for me as a Christmas gift. I'd worn it daily—my talisman, their love close to my skin while

I worked. Sadness showed up then to sit with me as I grasped how alone I feared I would feel for the next week.

I forced myself to continue reading my e-book. Normally, I put my phone on the floor as I flip my head upside down to finish blow drying my hair, flipping the pages with my toes. Usually, this is all the visual clue that Harley, my Heinz-57 dog, needs to rush over, tail wagging, to beg for love and attention.

This morning, however, she did not get up or raise her head. It was too early even for her. Without moving her head, she lifted her gaze upwards and at an angle as if exasperated that I was making such noise this early in the morning. If she could talk, I imagined her saying, "Woman, you're crazy. This is insane. Go back to bed."

For a split second, I considered cancelling the whole trip, though I knew I wouldn't get my payment back. Leaving the kids at my parents' house last night had been much more difficult than I'd imagined, their tears and pleas not to leave still fresh wounds in my heart.

I remembered my therapist's response to me after telling him about this retreat, his voice in my head as if he were in the same room with me. He had told me how good this was going to be for me, an invaluable tool in my recovery. So, I drummed up the necessary courage and finished drying my hair.

As I was attaching the clasp on my tiny heart pendant, my watch caught the chain as I was bringing my arm down to my side. I felt the necklace go slack and watched it fall to my feet.

I picked it up and saw that the chain had snapped. The opening inside the heart charm was too narrow for any other chain—just big enough for the original one, not a clasp.

Panic erupted in my chest as I started to look for anything that I could use to allow me to wear it again. I found some elastic, but it was a little too large at the frayed end to easily go through the small tunnel inside the charm.

I could feel the rage start to surge and a deep guttural roar flew out from the depth of my chest like that of a lion. Sam looked a little nervous as I continued to let it all emanate from my vocal cords.

I kept working at it, determined to fix it. Persistence is a virtue of mine, even when it outlasts its usefulness. Sam had offered to help, but I was too angry to accept help now.

After several more minutes, I realized that I was not going to be ready in time if I kept this up. The driver that Sam had hired to take us to the airport was to arrive in ten minutes. I finally relented and let Sam try.

I was sure this was a sign that I shouldn't go. This had to be a bad omen, but I was stuck. I couldn't back out now. It was too late.

Within minutes, Sam had the elastic through the heart. I tied several knots in the elastic and wore it as a bracelet. I held the tiny heart on the inside of my wrist and closed my eyes, summoning my kids' love.

I couldn't see the mess that I was in. I couldn't step aside to fully witness how much I looked like a wild animal, cornered and snarling, unable to see that the whole world was not a threat. I had learned to filter life through a lens of suffering but didn't know it was there.

CHAPTER 7

The Weight of Leaving

THE RIDE TO THE airport was quiet and dark, no one talking at all. I was a little light-headed, as the caffeine hit my empty stomach. I zoned out while watching the lights of a sleeping city go by.

We checked our luggage in with the skycap, proceeding onward to the TSA line. I'm always amazed at how many people there are in line this early in the morning. Our flight was at 5:55am and so we got there at 4:45am.

As we neared the front of the line, my mind flashed with another image of the kids and sadness once again enveloped me. Panic settled in as tears started to well up. I squatted down in line and tried to take a few deep breaths to help calm myself.

Sam leaned over and started to rub my back, "Are you okay?"

I stood up again and turned towards him. "I already miss the kids so much," I admitted. "Do you think they will be fine?"

He reassured me, but I could hear myself push back. He always thinks everything is going to be all right.

It was always me—the one who had to hold everything together, the one who made it all okay. What if I missed something? What if something unexpected happens? What if I hadn't done enough? My mind raced in circles like a dog chasing its own tail.

Thankfully, the line moved, and a TSA agent was directing us towards the scanners, asking us to put our personal items into the bins. At least this gave my mind something else on which to focus.

We moved through TSA quickly and found our gate. I watched the people around us as we sat. With a layover in Orlando, Florida, there were a lot of families around us buzzing with energy and anticipation. I wished I could have felt that too.

I had downloaded several books and music onto my phone to pass the time during our flights. Onboard, I started playing my favorite playlist and got into my book, only pulling my attention away when the plane would tilt and turn. I had to look out of the window to let my eyes see what my body could feel as we turned so that I wouldn't feel queasy.

We landed in Orlando and only had a little time before our next flight. Thankfully, our gate for the next flight wasn't far away.

The sun was up now. It's funny how things seem a little less frightening in the light. Plus, I was in travel mode—focused and present. There was no time to reminisce or worry. This was a blessing.

I refilled my caffeine and ate some more pretzels. I hadn't eaten before I left and my stomach started to growl ferociously.

CHAPTER 8

The Gulf of Hope

DURING THE LAST HALF of the flight, I noticed that we were flying over the Gulf of Mexico. Every now and then, the clouds would clear quite a bit, revealing a beautiful array of blue, teal, and turquoise water below.

For a moment, something lifted.

Grief had evaporated.

It wasn't gone for good, but it gave me space to breathe—space to notice the view beneath us. I never got tired of seeing bodies of water this way. Perhaps it is because I was born and raised in a landlocked state far from the tropics, but I am so indescribably drawn to this landscape.

Thirty minutes later, I noticed a vibrant green popping into view outside the window. Through the thin clouds, I could make out land. It was mountainous and deeply green everywhere.

I had no idea how many mountains and volcanos this country had. I remembered reading that Costa Rica had been created millions of years ago when the Caribbean and Cocos tectonic plates collided and continued to do so for over fifty million years. Volcanoes formed, erupted and pushed the land up.

I had been to Colorado and had seen mountains before, but never with rain forests. In fact, I had never seen a rain forest. I couldn't stop staring. The color, depth and complexity of the landscape as we grew nearer to the surface was dazzling. I didn't want to blink and miss even a second.

I tried to take pictures while we were descending, but the grey clouds above filtered the light. None of my photos came close to capturing what my eyes were seeing.

We landed and collected our luggage quickly so that we could go through customs. This was the next spike in anxiety. Customs always makes me nervous even though I know I'm not smuggling anything.

I don't know Spanish. Communication is never easy.

Sam and I walked up in front of a kind-looking woman behind a thick piece of plexiglass, with only a little mouse-sized hole through which to speak. It was nearly impossible to hear her, given the background noise. It reminded me of that old game telephone—the customs agent started the message.

By the time the message reached my ears, it had been warped by plexiglass, ambient sound, and her thick accent.

She asked about our purpose in coming to her country. I responded by telling her about the veterinary conference. She looked puzzled and said something to me. I'm still not sure if she actually used her voice or just mouthed the words.

For a moment, I got a preview of what it might feel like to grow old and hard of hearing. I finally understood the frustration.

She shook her head and asked, "Where are you going in Costa Rica?"

"Ohhhh," I froze. My mind went blank. It was like the file cabinet in my brain, where all my knowledge is kept, suddenly slammed shut and locked.

I fumbled for my phone, trying to open the email with the name of the town—but I couldn't get online. Chrome told me I wasn't connected to Wi-Fi.

As I started muttering to myself, wondering how I would figure out the name of the town, Sam moved forward. Speaking into the mouse hole, he said, "We're going to Co-**BAN**-oh."

She recoiled as if we had told her we were going to hell. So, Sam pulled up the text that I'd sent him with the address on his phone and showed her through the plexiglass.

"Ohhhh, **CO**-ban-oh," she replied, as if that cleared everything up.

I know enough to keep my face neutral, but in my mind I was doing some serious eye-rolling. This conversation had dragged on for about five to seven minutes, and I was starting to worry we might spend the entire week standing at that window. I half-expected to live out *The Terminal*, Tom Hanks-style. We eventually passed through customs and moved on to baggage claim.

We asked someone where to find Costa Rican Green Airways. We were told to leave the airport and walk down the street. Wait—walk down the street? That's not how airports work! Thank god I wasn't alone. I would have been freaking out if I'd had to figure that out by myself.

We stepped out into the bright hot sun wearing long pants and sweatshirts. The humid air hit us instantly—thick and clinging. If not for the constant breeze from passing cars and strong winds, it would've been unbearable.

As we walked to our left, we could see the much smaller domestic airport a half a block away. I felt better seeing our destination. Just inside the doors was a large hall with three to four airline counters. We moved towards the one for Costa Rican Green Airlines.

A smiling young woman asked how she could help us in nearly perfect English. I handed her our itinerary and she checked us in. After doing so, she asked Sam to step on the scale with his luggage.

He handed me his backpack and sweatshirt but she immediately stopped him, "You have to weigh yourself with everything you're carrying on."

That's when it hit me. We were flying on a really tiny plane--a baby plane-lette.

Then, it was my turn. I hate being weighed. I flashed back to my childhood—my grandmother picking my sister and me up from school, feeding us snacks and then leading us onto her husband's old physician's scale to weigh us. I would get lectured about my weight every school day. The memory of this has continued to haunt me to this day. I scolded Sam for looking at the numbers.

After that, we were good to go around the corner where there was a little snack shop. It was around 1:30pm and, aside from two little bags of pretzels, I hadn't had anything else to eat. So, I ordered an empanada and a water. We found the only two available seats near a large window that amplified the heat radiating in.

As I started to eat my empanada, there were two doe-like eyes staring up at me longingly. It was a golden retriever in a harness embroidered with the words 'support animal' on the side. The dog's name was Rosie and, much like the rest of her breed, she loved food. She was also quite proficient in using those eyes to win her edible prizes. As it turns out, it's quite difficult to eat a meal in front of an animal knowing you can't give them food. As hungry as I was, eating in front of Rosie without sharing was quite difficult.

Just then, Sam overheard our names being called. "I think we're boarding," he said to me.

I looked down at my watch and noticed that it was only 2:30pm. "But our flight doesn't leave for another hour. That can't be right," I replied.

A minute later, the disembodied voice from the loudspeaker called our names again. "See? I told you," he said, motioning for me to follow him. "I think we are boarding now."

I followed him to the check in gate. The same smiling woman from the check-in counter asked us for our wooden boarding passes. We waited for the last three passengers, Rosie and her two owners, before walking in single file out onto the tarmac.

We stood in line like a bunch of first graders eagerly awaiting further instructions from our teacher. Standing in queue, we waited for a jet to cross in front of us on the way to the runway. Within minutes, we boarded the little plane-lette, hoisting ourselves up the wobbly airstairs.

We boarded at the back of the plane where there was a large cooler filled with water and beer for us. The aisle was so narrow that I had to rotate my body to avoid hitting my hip on the seats, ducking my head as I moved. Being five foot three inches tall, I've never had to duck my head anywhere except when crawling through a McDonald's play area following one of my kids.

I buckled my seat belt and within minutes, we were speeding down the runway. I looked at my watch and noted that it was 3pm—a half hour early. During take-off, we banked and suddenly there was a perfect rainbow over the horizon of San Jose. I quickly opened my camera to capture it before the wings of the plane blocked my view. I saw this as a sign of good things to come.

About ten minutes later, we flew over a peninsula. The landscape shifted—green mountains gave way to turquoise blue waters. I took picture after picture hoping to capture all that I saw.

As we flew, I could hear one of the passengers behind me talking to Rosie's owners about going to see her daughter and granddaughter, who had just had a baby. Her daughter had started a business in Costa Rica working with horses—something about equine energy healing.

Not long after, the pilot let us know that we would be landing in Cobano shortly. I was expecting another airport similar to the one we had just left. Instead, we were met by a short, narrow runway and a small building.

The wind tossed our plane like a leaf, as it dipped, tilted and fluttered all the way down. At one point, I was holding my phone to play a card game and the plane dropped so suddenly that my arms and phone were suddenly thrust up into the air. I burst into laughter at how silly I must have looked. Apparently, I was the only one who thought it was funny.

After landing, we waited on the runway for the pilots to take our luggage out. Then, we walked up the ramp to the one room simple structure. It looked like a very small bus station. Inside, there were several cab drivers offering rides, but Jeremy had already arranged a ride for us. So, we decided to walk out the front door where we were met by even more taxi drivers. One was holding a small poster with my name written across it. I've only seen this in the movies. I felt so important. This person was looking for me specifically so that he could be of service to me. For once, I wasn't the one coordinating everything. I didn't have to ask, explain, or manage—it just happened.

Someone had shown up for *me*.

CHAPTER 9

The Road to Wild Sun

THE DRIVER WAS AN older gentleman who offered to take my luggage, but wouldn't take no for an answer. So, I walked myself to the SUV across the dirt road. His English was not great, but we could easily get the basic messages to each other on our ride to Cabuya. There was a simple beauty in the dirt roads edged by meadows, some with Brahman cows. I saw quite a few meadows speckled with these large white-ish cows with large dewlaps and the sweetest drooping ears. Soon, we were turning at a fork in the road and could see more zinc roofed cinder block homes and simple looking cemeteries along with little grocery stores. As we got closer to the beach of the Nicoya Bay, I could start making out a rocky shore and the water. I started getting excited. The driver weaved around the muddy roads. He explained that he was avoiding the large pits in the road. These roads were very narrow and yet, we would see large delivery trucks and vans moving through oncoming traffic as if there were plenty of room for four lanes of cars. People instinctively knew how to stop to let someone by and they would honk if they were going around another car going the same direction. Watching this made me a little nervous as the roads were winding and hilly. You couldn't see if oncoming traffic was close. After driving on these roads, I decided that I could never again complain about the roads back in Kansas City.

We hit a long straight stretch of road, an oddity here, and I glanced to my right through the window and saw a sign that read "Horse Spirit Healing". I immediately slapped Sam's upper arm and excitedly pointed to the sign explaining the connection to the passenger from our flight. I thought nothing of it then—just a neat connection. However, sometimes the universe plants something in your path before you know how much you'll need it.

We made a couple of turns eventually leading us up the hillside turning into the entrance for Wild Sun Rescue. I had no idea what to expect as the SUV edged through the narrow mud path lined with open air huts. There were a few people milling around both inside and outside. The trees (palm, banana, mango) created a canopy, shading us as we drove, slowly stopping at a small clearing next to a shed. We got out of the car and paid the driver in US dollars as he was talking to someone who worked for the rescue. We bid goodbye to our driver as Manuel introduced himself to us offering to carry my luggage to our room. I tried to argue, but he would have none of it as he guided us past the infinity pool overlooking the exotic greenery. It was a little cooler higher up in the jungle and the sun was sitting lower on the horizon than it was earlier in the day. I hadn't thought about the fact that the sun rises and sets at around 5:30am and pm due to being so close to the equator.

We were told to meet out by the pool in fifteen to twenty minutes where we would have a welcome meeting. I was not very confident in settings where I knew no one. So, I was glad to have Sam with me as it gave me someone to talk to if it got awkward. We walked into our room, surrounded by tropical vegetation, and immediately turned on the air conditioner. It was already set to 26 degrees Celsius. I had to google the conversion to Fahrenheit to learn that this was almost 79 degrees Fahrenheit. I immediately told Sam that it was too hot. I switched the conversions to see what 70 degrees equated to in Celsius. I discovered two things in this search. First, we needed to set it to 21 degrees Celsius to make it comfortable for us and, second, I have obviously never spelled out the word Fahrenheit before as I had no clue the third letter was an "h". As people are always expressing when learning something new, "I was 47, almost 48 years old when I realized this."

We settled in and unpacked some toiletries before leaving to walk the roughly fifty feet to the pool area. There, under a canopy, were a few others sitting at a table with seven glasses of white wine in assorted champagne and wine glasses. Galina, the retreat business owner, stood and walked over to us. She introduced herself and asked to hug me. Instantly, I felt a sense of safety and belonging. I had emailed her back and forth several months ago when I had initially started thinking that I needed to sign up for this retreat. I was terrified about taking the time off, of spending the money to come here, of leaving my children and of admitting to myself that I needed to do this for my mental and physical health. She had talked me off the ledge in those emails and was so eternally patient with me. She was around my age and height with medium blonde shoulder length curls. When she spoke, I could faintly hear the Canadian accent that I was accustomed to hearing from the two veterinary technicians that worked with me. She had actually lived in London, Ontario where one of my technicians lives. She handed Sam and me glasses of wine and gestured for us to sit down as others slowly made their way over.

After all seven of us were seated, Galina started to introduce Jeremy, the owner of the wildlife rescue and condos in which we were staying. He started off by going through some basics. We could take as many pictures as we wanted of the wildlife, but it was against the law for us to take pictures of wildlife if they were being handled. He explained that the volunteers who worked here were trained to shield the animals from non-volunteers to prevent any unauthorized pictures that may get them shut down permanently. He also explained that toilet tissue could not be flushed and had to be disposed of in the trash can. It's amazing how simple instructions like that were astonishingly difficult to execute after decades of throwing all tissue into the toilet. But I digress. Lastly, if we were going to bring food back into the rooms, we had to make sure it was covered or put away in bags or the room fridge as the ants here were dedicated to finding said food. So, if we didn't want to have an army of ants live with us for the week, we needed to strictly adhere to this one. As long as they didn't have palmetto bugs the size of my foot here, I was not worried about ants and other little insects.

CHAPTER 10

The Circle of Sanctuary

NEXT, WE WENT AROUND to make our introductions and tell the group why we were here. The first to speak was Sonja, our seminar instructor. She started by telling us that she had spent years working as an ER doctor and recounting her experiences with fatigue, highly stressful caseloads, demanding clients and the emotional, mental and physical toll it took on her. As she spoke, tears rolled down my cheeks silently—my face flushed, heart pounding. With every word she spoke, it sounded like she was looking into my depths and speaking about my own feelings. All of it resonated so much and I was so ill-prepared to shield these strangers from my emotions, as it happened so quickly. Next, Tammy, a relief veterinarian from Hawaii, spoke. Then Lindsay, Tammy's friend and colleague who moved back to the mainland years ago, spoke. With each of their stories, I could feel their pain, exhaustion, and frustration. I couldn't stop the tears. They continued to flow in recognition of shared pain as well as in response to the call for help. I was so deeply saddened that these good and loving veterinarians felt what I felt. Then, it was my turn.

"Hi. I'm Sarah. I'm a small animal veterinarian and have been working in this profession for twenty-three years. I did an internship after graduation in Atlanta, before returning home to Kansas City. I worked for two different clinics before deciding to start my own mobile clinic.

"At one point, about seven months after having my second child, I sought help from my therapist, thinking I was going through delayed postpartum depression. After a few sessions, he told me he didn't think it was postpartum at all—he believed I was reacting to a toxic work environment.

"So, I quit. I took three months off to build my mobile clinic from scratch. Within six weeks of opening, I found out I was pregnant. Eight weeks later, I turned forty. My clinic was still operating in the red.

"Then, being the English bulldog that I am—stubborn, driven, and apparently destined for repeat c-sections—I had my third one and made phone calls to clients during my four-day hospital stay. I saw clients at my house during my two-week maternity leave and even took the baby with me to a euthanasia appointment.

"From the time she was three weeks old until six weeks, she was on the truck with me. I was still nursing her between the handful of appointments I had each day.

"That was eight years ago. I've fought hard and persisted the entire time.

"But now? I don't have much left to give. I'm exhausted and burned out and scared to admit all of this to anyone—because I carry so much shame."

I spoke through tears and tried to control my voice with no success. I could see all the sympathetic eyes on me and felt their concern. Galina thanked all of us for being authentic and sharing our stories with the group. She then told each of us to take a chocolate from the Tupperware filled with different types of chocolates and enjoy. She spoke about her story and, though it is not mine to share, I can only say that the most beautiful souls on earth are often the ones with the most tremendously painful scars. It is because they've gone through such horrors that they want to help heal others. They often can't stand to see pain in others and will do anything to prevent the same pain they've experienced from touching another. I remember reading that this is why Robin Williams loved comedy so much. He knew what it felt like to hurt and he never wanted anyone else around him to feel that same way. So, he tried to make everyone smile or laugh. I understood that kind of ache—the drive to protect others from a pain you know too well. These are the most beautiful people on the planet. Whenever I'm in the presence of such souls—or even just reading about them—I can feel my heart almost ripping out of my chest.

Their pain—their beauty—leaves a footprint on my soul.

I didn't expect to find sanctuary in the circle—but that's exactly what it became.

CHAPTER 11

The First Exhale

WE ALL RETREATED TO our rooms for a little while before returning to the same area to have dinner together. In just forty-five minutes of sharing our stories, I felt so comfortable around these people that I had just met. I was looking forward to having dinner with everyone. This was new for me, and it made me smile. I could feel myself relax more with each minute I spent here. We ate our dinners at 7pm each night under the canopy and outdoor white lights. However, it was only Sonja, Tammy, Lindsay, Sam and I for dinner. We were served the most delicious fish, with black beans and a fresh salad. We had glasses of what looked like pale orange juice or even pineapple juice, but it was actually starfruit juice. I'd never had starfruit and had no expectations for how light, sweet and exotic it tasted. It was like I had suddenly woken from a coma and tasted food for the first time. Thinking back, I couldn't remember the last time I'd taken real pleasure in tasting food—*really* tasting it. It was like nothing I had ever experienced despite the fact that there was nothing fancy about it. The fish was caught this morning and all of it, the refried beans and salad as well, was bursting with flavor like we were eating in a Michelin 5-star restaurant. It was like my senses were slowly coming back into existence. The conversation was fun and lively, which made the dinner even more pleasurable and allowed us to get to know more about each other than just the painful parts. We were like puzzles pieces, once scattered, now slowly finding their way into place.

We finished dinner and bid each other good night, but not before Sonja told us that the yoga sessions were being moved to 6:30am instead of 7am. Prior to arriving in Costa Rica, I had promised myself that I was going to get up and do yoga every day as part of my healing process. I was absolutely not a morning person and dreaded getting out of bed early in the morning. I had become a snoozer at some point in my twenties and had started checking my email in bed each work day to delay leaving the coziness and security of my berth. So, this was a gargantuan request for me. It was 8:30pm and I was going to have to get ready for bed and try to get to sleep shortly if I were going to be made to rise with the sun for yoga. This might be a deal breaker.

As we walked back to the condo, I looked up at the blackness which was speckled with sparkling stars and planets. There was no light pollution here and so the stars were not shy, showing themselves in all their splendor. Sam and I walked up the spiral staircase to the top level of the condo where there was a lookout deck and a futon couch and chair. I pulled out my phone, opening my sky view app to see that it was Jupiter, the brightest star in the northern sky. There was a stillness and peace that I felt leaning on the banister of the deck almost 3200 miles away from my home. The distance was protective, preventing me from worrying about work and the kids as well as from the relentless need to constantly be doing. It was the first time in a long time I didn't feel responsible for everything and everyone. I slowly walked back down the shallow spiral staircase to my room, leaving my shoes outside before opening the sliding glass door to ready myself for bed.

I wasn't sure what tomorrow would bring—but for the first time, that didn't scare me.

CHAPTER 12

A Gift From the Universe

Monday, December 9th: *I am waking up in the jungle in Costa Rica. As the sun is rising over the Gulf of Nicoya spilling into the Pacific Ocean, I can hear the sounds of the jungle waking up. The deep, guttural, and almost barking sounds of the howler monkeys follow in a cyclical pattern punctuated by the squawks and screams of the scarlet macaws. The ambient songs of the smaller birds sprinkled throughout. This chorus lasts several seconds before pausing, only to repeat indefinitely. It was 5:30am and never before had I had the urge to leap out of bed to go watch the sunrise, beating my alarm clock. The light streaming in around the curtains made it feel so much later. I grabbed my phone and glasses and quietly snuck out the sliding glass door leading onto the deck overlooking the bay. Out over the horizon, the sun would shortly make her quotidian debut. There are some semi-translucent clouds in the sky against the baby blue background. Beneath that, the* grayish white clouds gradually change to more of a gray-yellow and then gold. As the sun begins her journey up, she has found an opening in the thicker clouds, peeking through. It feels like this spectacular show is being put on just for me—like the universe knows how badly I needed to rediscover wonder. As she crests the clouds, I can see the crepuscular rays radiate outward in a dazzling display. It is as though the animals of the jungle are calling out to the sun begging her to come play. I have taken so many pictures of the sunrise knowing that I would never again see such a display, nor would I probably be so willing to wake so early. It is like the air is infused with caffeine. Oddly, I am not the least bit tired, despite only getting a couple of hours of sleep before leaving town the day before.

I keep hearing of the magic that can be found down here and I'm optimistic that I can find answers as though I'm visiting the great and powerful Oz. I feel like I'm at a crossroads of sorts and don't know what paths even lie ahead. I feel both anticipation and excitement as well as fear, both fear of having to make a choice but also fear that no options will appear before me. I don't know what lies ahead. I'm very excited to learn more about everything that these next few days will bring. But they also mentioned play. I think that is a key thing that I forget to do. I know I play with my children—but maybe the kind of play I need looks different. Maybe it's what brings me back to myself. When I've shed the layers of myself that are not really me, maybe I will learn what type of play truly suits me. For now, I will do yoga each morning.

I will try to be open to everything without fear or the need to hide. I welcome the opportunity to change. As Brene Brown says, "I'm going to choose discomfort for now in order to avoid resentment later."

CHAPTER 13

Strength
Becoming Stillness

IT WAS A LITTLE after 6am and I needed to change clothes and get ready for yoga. I did so without turning the lights on so as to not wake Sam, who had zero intentions for doing any sort of yoga at 6:30am.

I snuck outside with my bug spray and coated myself in it, creating an invisible shield for any insect within close proximity. I slipped on my flip-flops on and walked past our outdoor dining space, past the clearing and storage shed—

and that's where I saw a large rodent-like creature.

Immediately, I thought of the fire swamps from *The Princess Bride* where they encountered the R.O.U.S. (rodents of unusual size) and giggled to myself that I was following one into the yoga platform.

Actually, it was an agouti.

They look like longer-legged, large guinea pigs and, like Alice following the white rabbit, I quietly followed him along the path as I headed towards the open air, thatched roof yoga platform. It was enshrouded with exotic vegetation making it feel very secluded. I was the first to arrive and so I left my flip-flops on the little wooden bridge to the platform. I walked around, taking in all the sounds and various shades of green foliage, hearing voices getting louder as the others showed up. Sonja came walking in with our yoga instructor, Linea. In addition to being an ER vet, Sonja was also a yoga instructor. Normally, I would have been a little self-conscious about being in class with more advanced practitioners, but I didn't feel any of that here. As the final few came onto the platform, Linea started playing soft music and welcomed us to sit in easy pose. In past yoga classes, we were expected to sit with one leg crossed on top of the other while sitting on top of our sit bones. However, this wasn't an easy pose for me, so I was happy to be able to sit like this for once. As we all sat there and tried to quiet our minds to allow us to hear and feel our bodies more, she told us to breathe in the oxygen from the jungle and breathe out all of what no longer served us.

With my eyes shut, I thought about everything I still carried—even though it no longer served me. Perfectionism, the feeling that I have to push myself so incredibly hard every waking moment or risk being labeled as a failure, fear of making mistakes, fear of disappointing anyone else, shame surrounding my body and the weight gain that came on so suddenly and ferociously at the start of perimenopause, thoughts that everyone else is harshly judging everything about me all the time, loneliness and the fear that it is due, in part, because there's something inherently wrong with me, just to name a few things that no longer serve me. These thoughts weighed me down as if I were carrying 999 chains, each attached to concrete blocks, trudging through life. As Linea asked us to take deep breaths from the depths of our bellies, I realized that these thoughts were also suffocating me, making it difficult to take anything but short little breaths. I could not expand my belly and diaphragm making it difficult to allow my lungs to fill to their capacity. As if she were seeing my thoughts above my head, Linea then told us that we had to be able to push our bellies out to be able to expand our lungs. She went on to tell us that we had to go against what had likely been programmed into our heads and allow our bellies to be soft rather than constantly tucked in. This was the only way to bring in the richness of the jungle air and start the healing process. She urged us to let the jungle have all our pain and sorrow. It could handle it.

As she gently guided us through all the yoga poses, I could feel my muscles start to fatigue and sweat started running down my face and hands, making it a little more difficult to keep my hands steady on the mat during down dog. Next, she asked us to lie on our backs and push our legs up in the air creating a ninety-degree angle at the hips while flexing our feet and holding our legs together. We lay like this for several minutes. She started walking around us as she told us that our legs and feet would likely start to shake and tremble. As she came by my feet, she placed her hand over the bottoms of both feet and said that this trembling was all the stress leaving our bodies. I don't know why, but this resonated with me. I could see and feel my trembling feet and legs as I visualized all of my stress energetically exiting my body out into the jungle. Linea went on to tell us that this was a good pose to do when we got home from work or at bedtime to release all the stress and worry from the day. I took a mental note of this. I really wanted to make this a daily practice. I might not be able to do sixty-minute yoga classes each day, but I could strike a pose (more yoga, less Madonna) for a few minutes each day and visualize letting go of my stresses. At this point, I had nothing to lose.

Closing out our practice for the day before ending in savasana or corpse pose, Linea asked us to stand up and fold our thumbs within our palms, circling our fingers around them.

This was Mushti Mudra. We closed our eyes.

First, we crossed our arms over our chest—then returned them to our sides. Then we lifted them overhead as if tossing something behind us. Again, arms to the sides. Then repeat.

She played a rhythmic drum track to guide our movements. As the beat pulsed around us, she told us that this sequence was about more than just building strength—it was about feeling our strength and releasing stress through motion.

I imagined myself as a warrior preparing for battle.

I did feel strong, but this feeling was not new to me.

I've long known that I am strong, mentally and physically. I have endurance.

But as the drums went on, my arms started burning. My shoulders ached. I wasn't sure how much longer I could keep going.

And for once, instead of forcing myself through it, I noticed it.

My body was tired. It wasn't failure—it was a message.

Maybe strength didn't mean pushing harder. Maybe it meant knowing when to pause.

Savasana or corpse pose is a very common way to end a yoga session. It was my favorite pose.

By the end of class, my muscles were fatigued and I was drenched in sweat.

The jungle breezes swept through the platform, allowing me to cool down quickly.

Linea started the final song. When I listen to songs, I instinctively listen to the music itself, separate from the lyrics. Lyrics often feel like poetry, and I never connected with poetry. I hated having to analyze it to extract symbolism I didn't feel. I felt like we were overreaching, interpreting meaning that wasn't there.

But music itself? Music evokes meaning without thought. It bypasses thought and speaks directly to my soul.

This melody was haunting. Beautiful.

I could feel all the dopamine wash over me, like waves. Goose-bumps rose along every inch of my skin.

Tears came quietly, without shame. My body, my breath, and my emotions were finally in sync—for the first time in a very long time.

As the breeze stirred again, cool against my sweat-soaked skin, I felt completely still.

There was no other place in the world I wanted to be.

CHAPTER 14

Recognizing the Fractured Life

WE WERE TREATED TO a breakfast of Belgian waffles and assorted tropical fruits and more starfruit juice. As we finished our breakfast, some of the others headed back to the condo for a little while before we started the seminar portion of the day. I was so relaxed and in the mood to soak everything in, that I decided to stay at the table for a little longer. Sonja and Galina had started to stand up when one of them, in a hushed tone, told me to look over towards the condo. At that moment, a deer popped out of the bushes and carefully walked out into the clearing, closely followed by her fawn. Galina whispered that she had twins, and the other fawn would be coming along soon. As the momma scanned her surroundings and carefully watched for any sudden movements, she led her fawn up towards a large bush at the other end of the clearing where we were sitting. At that moment, the other fawn popped out of the bushes trying to catch up.

As humans, we tend to move through the world as if we own it.

It was different here. This land belonged to the animal and plant life here. We were merely guests in their home—witnessing the serenity.

In the stillness of the moment, the doe guided her babies through the brush, trusting us to witness their world.

I realized that it was the pause where time seemed to expand, allowing me to find beauty and magic right then.

Maybe beauty isn't hidden–we're just too busy to notice its simplicity.

After the deer passed, I walked back to the condo to grab our seminar workbooks, my journal, my water and my crossbody bag. Then I headed back over to the yoga platform where the morning seminar would begin.

I was genuinely looking forward to it. I felt lighter. Hopeful. Feelings I hadn't touched in a very long time.

I was desperate to release the heaviness that comes with having to be everything for everyone. It was a weight I hadn't realized I was still carrying until I finally started to put it down.

I was barely surviving, overwhelmed and exhausted—this wasn't living.

I yearned to feel alive again.

If I had to write a job description for what I felt were my duties, it would include:

- Be the best veterinarian I can be—caring for both the physical and emotional needs of my patients and their owners.

- Do tasks my clients could do themselves, so they don't have to.

- Work until the job is done, not when the workday ends.

- Research cases after hours.

- Raise my children—make sure they're dressed, fed, getting to school, doing their homework, and getting help if they're struggling.

- Monitor their emotional well-being and advocate for them in school and life, teaching them to be kind, responsible, emotionally intelligent humans.

- Care for the animals in our home.

- Keep the house clean.

- Do the grocery shopping.

- Stay in therapy and heal from childhood trauma.

- Break the cycle of generational pain—so my children never have to carry it.

This was not an exhaustive list either, as I'm sure I was forgetting some duties. Just thinking of it was tiresome.
Living it had nearly broken me.
I often felt like one of those circus performers who had to keep the plates spinning on the sticks--only mine were constantly crashing down, no matter how fast I ran between them.
In the face of failure, I persist rather than pivot.
I thought this was how we show strength, but my frustration

was born out of this behavior. I'd confused survival for strength—
believing that enduring without complaint was noble, even when
it was slowly breaking me.

And I couldn't see that I was the one setting all the plates
spinning in the first place.

CHAPTER 15

The Caretaker and the Imposter

WE CAME INTO THE yoga platform and sat at the two tables that were set out facing a large screen. Sonja and Galina were there trying to get the computer set up to share the screen. Sam had come with me and sat in between me and Lindsay.

Once we were all seated and situated, Sonja asked us to select a question card from her pile. We each chose a card and answered to help us learn a little more about each other.

Lindsay's question asked what she did to help her calm down when she was feeling overwhelmed. She told us about one of her favorite songs, Lark Ascending—a joyfully pastoral piece with a solo violin playing over the soft swell of an orchestra behind it.

Sonja asked us to open our workbooks and start a writing exercise asking us to remember why we wanted to become veterinarians and then ask if our professional lives were the same as what we had once dreamed of. I thought back to that day that I watched the puppy that my sister and I had gotten on Christmas Eve when I was eight years old.

She had run across the street to see people walking on the other side when she got run over by both the front and back passenger wheels of the newspaper delivery van.

She died instantly as I stood at my bedroom window, screaming as I watched in horror before sinking down in tears, knowing that there was no way she could have survived.

That experience cemented my desire to try to heal animals. I had always loved animals. At that point in my life, I had only met animals who were gentle and eager to love me. I knew that I wanted to be a clinical veterinarian like the ones to whom we had taken our dogs. At that point, I didn't know that there was any other way to use a degree in veterinary medicine, other than to work on large animals, which I didn't want to do. Thinking back to the beginning of my career, a lot has changed, but a lot has not. I was dealing with imposter syndrome throughout my time in vet school. I constantly questioned my competence, certain that my classmates knew more than I did—even when my grades didn't reflect that. The more I learned, the more I realized how much I didn't know. As the years went on and graduation loomed near, I was in a near panicked state daily. I had assumed that by my fourth and final year in school, I would have felt much more confident in my knowledge and able to work as a competent veterinarian. When I didn't feel this way, I just knew that there was something wrong with me. With each rotation through the various specialties (anesthesia, small animal medicine, surgery, pathology, equine medicine/surgery, etc), I kept getting reviews from my senior clinicians that said my confidence was too low and I was going to have to work on that. In our first year, one of our professors told us that vet school would teach us how to learn, but that the real learning would come on the job. I don't think I realized how much information I would soak up in four years and yet still feel so inadequate.

CHAPTER 16

The Master Litigator

SOCRATES IS CREDITED WITH saying, "The only true wisdom is in knowing you know nothing." Science and medicine are always changing due to new discoveries and a better understanding of our world, nature and the human body. However, evolution and mutation make it impossible to know everything. Yet, I came out of vet school beating myself up for not knowing everything. This did little to enhance my already-low self-confidence, but rather worsened my imposter syndrome. I didn't realize at the time how common this was—I just thought it meant I wasn't cut out for this.

Back then, imposter syndrome was not widely known. I was ashamed and didn't talk about how I felt.

Had I spoken up, I would have learned that I was not alone.

The estimates suggest that at least 70 percent of the population experience these symptoms at some point in their lives.

I assumed that with time and experience, my confidence would grow as my knowledge did. Little did I realize that this wouldn't prove to be true.

Any counterarguments made in my head, regarding my

accomplishments, were quickly met with the belief that my achieve-ments were all due to sheer luck or to external factors outside of my control.

That critical voice in my head was a master litigator—it always won. I could never win. The voice that told me I wasn't enough had endless evidence—and a ruthless tone.

A large part of my anxiety stems from not knowing. Will I have the answers to the questions my clients ask? Will I be able to solve and treat my patients' ailments with whatever, if any, diagnostics I'm allowed to run?

The inner critic loves to tell me that all other vets would be able to do so.

In journaling out these questions, I started to realize how I had created a co-dependent and toxic relationship with my profession. I have always felt this career path was a calling—something sacred—carrying an enormous sense of duty. I thought giving everything made me a good vet. But it just made me disappear.

As I learn to become more self-aware, I can see now that I had been using my clients' and patients' gratitude and love to fulfill an emptiness inside. Once I got that validation, it soothed something raw and unhealed in me—and I didn't want to lose that.

So I worked harder. I did more. I gave and gave until there was nothing left for myself.

I was so willing to do whatever seemed necessary that I failed to realize that I was giving too much without refueling myself, often at the cost of family time. I could feel myself disappearing.

These self-imposed feelings—having to do everything myself and always exceed everyone's expectations—seemed to protect me from the fear of feeling like a failure, stupid and unworthy of my degree.

I could feel resentment building inside my chest.

At first, it was slow. But in recent years, it's ramped up with a frantic pace, leaving me drained and angry at myself.

I had worked so hard for so many years to outrun this cavernous sense of unworthiness, only to realize that I was killing myself.

I was no closer to feeling worthy of bearing the letters DVM behind my name than when I started.

And now, I was exhausted as well.

CHAPTER 17

Out of Alignment

THE FINAL QUESTION FOR our journals at that point asked what mattered most to us in our lives today. For me, this was the easiest question of all.

Though cliché, I have always felt that my role as mother to my three children was the hardest and possibly the most important one that I will ever fill.

There has always been so much generational trauma that has spilled down through so many branches of our family tree. I made a pact with myself, years prior to ever taking that first pregnancy test, that the trauma would end with me.

I was fortunate to have entered adulthood at the commencement of the age of the internet, allowing me access to the knowledge and tools that previous generations did not have.

I truly believe that one of the main purposes in my life is to halt all of that trauma that has coursed through our family like a freight train, preventing it from ever touching my children.

If nothing else, I know that I've made progress. I'm teaching my children what my generation—and those before me in our family—never had the tools to learn: how to create boundaries, build emotional intelligence, and develop a sense of agency.

I'm immensely proud of this.

I've worked hard to heal what was wounded within me, so it doesn't bleed into another generation.

It suddenly dawned on me—

Even though I was writing about my children mattering the most, and my life's purpose as a cycle breaker being my greatest calling,

I wasn't acting in alignment with those truths. Not at all.

For financial reasons, I had to work. We needed a two-person household income.

For many years, I truly loved working. I got a thrill when I could work through a case, meet a new patient who would cover me in wet kisses or see that I was making a difference in the lives of my clients and patients.

I was quite good at it. I built strong relationships with my clients. I educated and reassured them. I made people feel heard—and their pets feel safe.

But somewhere along the way, I stopped knowing *why* I was still doing it.

Was I staying in clinical practice due to a deep sense of duty–or because I still loved it?

As I asked myself that question, fear filled my chest, rising into my throat.

I quickly scribbled in my workbook, *I'm scared that my path may be leading me to leave either clinical practice or the profession altogether.*

The truth of this statement brought more guilt and shame. But I knew that I could no longer afford to ignore this.

Sarah Burkindine

I needed time—not just to reflect, but to be honest with myself.

CHAPTER 18

Walking Through Wild Sun

AFTER LUNCH, WE TOOK a tour of the rehab facility on the grounds of which we were staying. There were several prefabricated domes scattered throughout the little jungle village, each with their own purpose (surgery, treatment, etc.). Open-air huts where the volunteers would eat and spend their down time, along with the kitchen, lined the main road through the facility. Everyone I knew who had been to Costa Rica told me how happy and kind the people were. That was definitely true here as well. Everywhere we turned, people were laughing or smiling as they worked. It was infectious. Even the breeding macaws, domesticated birds who were confiscated from illegal trading sources and cannot be introduced into the wild, seemed happy and relaxed here.

The tour ended at the entrance to the rescue facility where we hopped into an old SUV and started out towards Montezuma to hike up to the waterfalls.

CHAPTER 19

Healing by Waterfall

IT WAS A TWENTY minute incredibly bumpy drive on a mud-packed road barely wide enough to fit two cars driving opposite one another. Between the deep pits in the mud, the mothers pushing strollers down the side of the road and avoiding cars randomly parked along the side, the serpentine path we took was lively to say the least. Jeremy, the owner of the rescue, pulled over to the side to let us out at the Montezuma waterfall trailhead. We started out following the stream up the gentle incline, paying attention to the slick spots where water was constantly rushing over small boulders and rocks. We followed Sonja and Galina at first, since they knew better than we did where we were headed. Not long after we started, we were met with a kind-looking older man who looked to be in his early 70's. His face was dark and worn like leather with wrinkles that only come with decades of smiling or laughing. His squinting eyes showed the happiness of the simplistic life he most likely led. In broken English, he pointed and told us where to step and held out his arm as a universal sign of assistance.

We accepted his arm and continued following him on the path.

As we hiked, he led us in a single file line like the little leaf-cutter ants that marched tirelessly alongside us, carrying leaves three times larger than their little bodies back to their colony. We found a rope banister to grab as we climbed back down the embankment to the stream where we could start to hear the gentle roar, increasing in volume as we neared. Within a few feet, we turned the corner to the right and saw the vast opening where not one, but two waterfalls poured into the expansive plunge pool below.

The first one I saw was large and booming, where the second was demure, hidden towards the back of the basin that stretched out before us. I found a large boulder on which to set my things so that I could submerge myself in the cool waters. It was 78 degrees Fahrenheit with a humidity around 75 percent and we were all glistening with sweat. The water was a cool, sweet relief like none I had ever felt. The buoyancy of the water took pressure off all my muscles, allowing me to fully relax into myself. Galina had floated over to where Sam, Sonja and I were wading. I turned to her and thanked her.

"I'm so sorry for all the emails and questions leading up to this trip. I was so entirely terrified of coming down here for this retreat. I've never done anything like this before and yet it was something I should have done a long time ago. This retreat has already done so much to alert me to what I had been neglecting in myself.

"It's been like CPR for my soul," I told her, as tears started to build up threatening to spill over the lower lids like the waterfalls behind us.

"I was where you are now just a few years ago. I know what you are going through. That's exactly why I wanted to do this," she said.

She went on to tell me how she had come down to Costa Rica for scuba diving and was at a crossroads. It was down here, in Costa Rica, where she begged the question, what next?. The universe had answered her. As she spoke, I sent a wish that it would send me answers as well. I felt like I had been pushing against a brick wall, solid and unmoving, for so long, expecting to break through it. I couldn't see any other paths—my forehead pressed against the wall—and all I could see was brick. I was so tired of applying futile force. I was exhausted and had very little energy left to keep going. Waves of fear would engulf me as I could not figure out what to do when the last bit of energy left my body. I felt like I had no one else to rely upon. Who would care for my children or my clients or me should that happen? It was the first time that I acknowledged to myself that I had limits to what I could do and how far I could go.

For the first time, I had stopped to consider that in thinking of myself as a horse, I was perpetually pushing myself past my own limits. Many horses will continue to push themselves for as long as the rider asks them to, until they collapse. Whereas, a mule will stop before they get to the point of exhaustion. I had always considered it a more honorable characteristic to be able to keep testing my own limitations.. However, I failed to realize that once a horse collapses, it takes an enormous amount of treatment to get that horse into working condition again, if at all possible. Is it not more intelligent to be like the mule who recognizes the limitations of the body, mind, and spirit?

I was starting to gain insight into just how debilitated I was, not only mentally, but physically and emotionally as well. I didn't think I was at the end of my rope yet, but I was close.

Galina brought out the watermelon slices that Chef had sent for us. As I took a bite from the fleshy pulp, the sweet juice running down the side of my mouth, I took a few moments to enjoy the magnificence of the waterfall roaring in front of me, feeling lucky that I was here. As the rest of our group slowly emerged from the water, Sonja suggested that we take a group picture in front of the waterfall.

A jolt of joy and belonging hit me as a smile naturally spread across my face.

Sam took several pictures of us before handing me the phone. Without thinking, I took a photo of myself with the waterfall over my left shoulder. Not one to take selfies, I suddenly wanted a picture of myself with the waterfall. I wanted a visual reminder of the subtle shift within me, wanting to capture not just the view, but the version of me who had made it here.

I didn't want to head back just yet, but there were more people showing up to see the falls and play in the water. It started to feel much more public and overwhelming to me.

As we walked through the streams past the larger boulders, someone was happily screaming out to his friends below him. He was dangling from his knees about 2 stories above the water off the edge of a branch before he let go and gracefully fell into the water below. The peals of laughter from the group of acrobatic friends rang out as someone else climbed the tree after him like a leopard, fast and nimble. Tammy or Lindsay suggested they may be performers of a Cirque de Soleil-like show. As we turned the corner and left the basin, I carried the moment with me—being here in these waters, surrounded by my newfound tribe.

We walked back guiding each other through muddy hills, slimy rock paths and slippery underwater footholds, each looking after the person behind her.

CHAPTER 20

The Emotional Tension of Healing

WE FOUND JEREMY'S SUV parked just to the side of the main road and piled in. On the way back, I watched through the window as the sights and sounds of Montezuma raced by through the window, noticing the peaceful contentment within me.

My muscles were tired from the hike and evaporation had started to cool me down as we opted for the air conditioning over open windows. I had also noticed that there was greater distance between my shoulders and my ears than ever before. I hadn't even known I was carrying them so high—until they dropped. I could feel the noticeable difference. A small smirk crept onto my lips with a flicker of pride. I had allowed my body to relax—maybe for the first time in a long while.

We made it back to the rescue center and condo well before dinner. With that time, I decided to work on the self-reflection exercises Sonja had asked us to do before tomorrow's session. We were asked to build strategies for self-care that we could easily incorporate daily. My initial reaction was to scoff at this. Who has the time to add one more thing to their day? My mind continued to provide evidence.

You can't get up earlier than 5:30am on workdays—you aren't a morning person.

You don't get home until 6 or 7 p.m. most nights, and then you have to help with dinner, get the kids to bed, and take care of yourself.

You would never be able to justify taking off an additional day during the week—or cutting more time out of your work day.

You're barely holding it together as it is. Adding more "self-care" sounds nice, but it's just not realistic.

Ignoring this inner voice, I treated it like homework, not self-care—checking boxes, not committing to change.

While staring at the list of suggested self-care practices, I turned inward to explore. I'd been introspective since childhood—it came easily to me. I've journaled on and off throughout my adult life, and I've always loved to write. So journaling was my top choice. It was a way for me to find my true self.

Through years of working with my therapist, I've learned to befriend the hurt child inside me—the one I kept hidden away for decades.

She was shielded by protective parts: the perfectionist, the harsh inner critic, the people-pleaser, the caretaker and the overthinker.

I've worked tirelessly to earn the hurt inner child's trust, to help heal her wounds.

I've never been afraid of negative emotions. I learned long ago that you can't experience joy without experiencing pain.

Maybe that's also why I hold space for others in their darkness—I'm not afraid of it. I've lived there myself.

Perhaps I have been doing self-care all along–it just wasn't enough.

I've always been a girl who loves air conditioning, so getting outside in the heat and humidity was never my thing. Spring and summer in Kansas City are beautiful—but short. But I had recently started gardening—not because I liked it, but because I liked what came from it. I'm not someone who loves playing in the dirt. But I do *love* having beautiful things to look at.

At first, it was about creating a space I could enjoy when I went outside. But soon, it became something else: a quiet, persistent responsibility.

This past summer, I watched as bumblebees floated in and out of my foxglove blooms—their fuzzy little butts disappearing into the petals. I'd never seen one before.

I felt like a toddler getting excited over seeing bubbles for the first time.

I wanted to get closer—touch them but settled for taking pictures and videos of them instead.

Maybe that's what this kind of self-care is. It's not about finding joy in the labor, but about making space for the magic that follows.

My therapist has recommended grounding for years.

I tried the visualizations—imagine you're a tree, your feet growing roots deep into the Earth—but it never really worked for me. I never felt anything.

So, I did what I always do when I don't understand something: I researched it.

That's where I learned about earthing, the idea that walking barefoot on natural ground allows your body to connect with the Earth's energy. Supposedly, it can reduce inflammation, regulate cortisol, even calm anxiety.

There's some science behind it, too. The National Institutes of Health has studies. That helped speak to the part of my brain that seeks evidence and logic.

And it made sense—humans used to walk barefoot and sleep

on the ground. But now? We're sealed off from the Earth by shoes, concrete, and houses. Maybe we've disconnected from something our bodies still need.

This knowledge helped uncover the barefoot hippie that's always lived quietly inside me. I've started slipping off my shoes when I'm outside with the kids. Sometimes I close my eyes, feeling the sun on my face, and time slows down again.

Meditation has always been difficult for me. I sit, eyes closed, expecting something powerful.

I envision a Buddhist monk in a silent trance for hours. I expect the same of my mind. Serenity. Stillness. Wisdom.

My mind, however, is more like a room full of angry chimpanzees grunting, hooting and barking all at once–a cacophony of noise.

I needed guidance to stay focused during meditation, helping to quiet the chimps.

I have several guided meditations that my therapist recorded for me. I can listen while I close my eyes—the warmth of the sun on my face and the coolness of the grass in between my toes.

This worked well for me, but inertia does make it difficult for me to seek time for this practice.

My therapist had introduced me to tapping—a technique that combines tapping on acupuncture points with spoken affirmations. It's used to redirect the mind and reset the nervous system.

However, I found myself incapable of coming up with spoken affirmations. The perfectionist in my head was too critical.

I found an app that guides you through the tapping process. I didn't have to come up with anything on my own—I just had to follow along. It was exactly what I needed.

I had started tapping ten minutes every workday before dropping the kids off at school. It did help lessen the severe anxiety. I viewed the world as emotionally unsafe. But, within my home and with my children, I was protected.

Perhaps I had been doing self-care all along. I just wasn't doing enough of it, or doing it with the awareness that I deserved it.

In the last few years, I have become very interested in psychology and how the mind works. I suspect that most of this is motivated by my own desire to understand my own mental and emotional patterns.

My therapist mentioned the word generational trauma and from that point on, I was like Alice following the white rabbit.

One article or book would lead to another and then another. I spiraled through research—watching Alan Watts' videos, listening to podcasts like Secular Buddhism and reading books about how trauma can cause disease.

After writing all of these down, I felt frustration start to build. I had been doing so much work already.

And yet… I was still here—burned out, emotionally drained, barely holding on. Facing myself in burnout, I felt like Clarice meeting Hannibal Lecter for the first time, afraid yet fascinated.

The little girl inside me was frightened and exhausted, without any sense of control.

The clinician in me wanted to understand the pathology, to diagnose and to cure.

Somnolence crept in, ready to take me. I set down my journal for the day, turned on my spa playlist, and gave myself permission to take my mind offline for the evening.

CHAPTER 21

Reclaiming My Power

I SLEPT LATER THE second morning I was there. The usual jungle sounds were hushed with the slowly moving rainstorm.

I stayed in bed longer listening to the sound of the rain rhythmically hitting the windows.

I reveled in the knowledge that I had nowhere to be and nothing to do at this moment. I have not felt this in a long time.

Even weekends came with chores and responsibilities at home. But here, I could simply be—nuzzled by my comforter, wrapped in stillness.

I could hear the squawking of the macaws outside, a sound that created excitement that splayed throughout my body. I had yet to capture their flight on video, though. As the rains lightened, I peeled myself out of bed to get ready to go to yoga.

Walking through light drizzle on my way to the yoga platform, I noticed the trees above me coming alive with capuchin monkeys. Their rustling was soft and familiar now.

I walked slowly with a sense of belonging—as if I had never known any other home but here.

I left my flip-flops at the entrance and started to get yoga mats out of the closet. One by one, Sonja, Lindsay and Tammy and Galina arrived, rolling out their mats near mine.

We sat, eyes closed, creating circles with our upper body. We learned how to synchronize our movements with our breath, deepening our connection with our bodies.

This gentle transition eased us into the morning's practice, inviting stillness into our minds.

I had not practiced yoga in many years. Vinyasa yoga was exhausting. I never could get into a rhythm where I would enjoy the practice. A few years ago, I tried restorative yoga, a more relaxing style focused more on deep relaxation and stress reduction. I truly enjoyed this form. However, I quit due to cost and the amount of time it took away from work and home life. I told myself it was selfish—to spend time or money on myself—when I could give it to my family instead.

This morning's class was invigorating and empowering. One of the last things we did before ending in savasana was to stand using the Adhi mudra—a symbolic hand gesture used to restore balance and inner peace.

With eyes closed, we curled our thumbs into our palms, wrapping our fingers around the thumb.

A steady drumbeat played in the background—no melody, just rhythm.

The sound helped guide our breath and movements, like a metronome for the body.

It reminded me of the drum corps in ancient battles—keeping soldiers in step, focused, unified. But here, the rhythm wasn't preparing us for destruction.

It was preparing us to reclaim ourselves.

This sequence was meant to build strength. Not just in our arms, but in our sense of self.

With each exhale, I threw something away—something heavy, something old.

With each inhale, I pulled myself back to center.

Over and over, for five full minutes.

I could feel my arms burning. My shoulders trembling.

But I also felt power rising in me.

Not power over anything or anyone else. Just the quiet, rooted power of being fully present in my own body.

As I lay in savasana, my body spent, I realized something:

I was stepping into my strength, my power.

I wasn't forcing anything.

I was reclaiming what had been deep within me all along.

I felt magnificent.

CHAPTER 22

The Language of Healing

THAT MORNING, SONJA INTRODUCED a new word I'd never heard before: *equanimity*.

She described it as the ability to remain grounded—even in the face of difficult emotions or stressful situations.

Not emotionless. Not numb. Just…steady, like a ship on calm waters.

It was the first time I had heard language put to something I had always struggled with.

I've read articles about the difference between reacting and responding. But this was different.

This was about staying present—choosing your response instead of being hijacked by the moment.

The next topic for discussion was centered around the idea of the window of tolerance. Within this window, our nervous system is working optimally. Here, we are emotionally regulated—we feel calm and relaxed. She then taught that trauma and stress will narrow this window, making it easier to tilt over into fight, flight, freeze or fawn modes. This is where we become emotionally dysregulated.

This is where things get scary, at least for me.

As Sonja spoke about the nervous system and the concept of the window of tolerance, I thought back to my childhood—and to my mother.

She was teaching full-time, going to school at night to earn her Educational Specialist degree, and driving me and my sister to activities in between. Her days were packed beyond reason.

She was trying to do it all and doing it under enormous pressure.

I can see now that her window of tolerance was narrow. Her patience was short, her stress constant. She was doing her best with what she had—but she was overwhelmed most of the time.

And when her nervous system tipped into a hyperaroused state, it could be terrifying.

As a child, I didn't have words for what I was seeing. I just knew that when she reached that point—anxious, angry, reactive—I wasn't safe.

I didn't know what would happen next. So I learned to anticipate it. I became very good at meeting her needs before she even asked. I learned to people please—not for praise, but for survival.

I could read the sound of her heels in the hallway. The jingle of her keys. Her sighs. The tone of her voice. Her silence.

I could feel her moods.

And for a long time, I thought this was normal. I don't believe she ever wanted to hurt me. But I still felt the pain nonetheless.

As I listened to Sonja describe how trauma can narrow our window of tolerance, I started seeing how hard I had been working to keep mine from being too narrow—for everyone else.

I had spent years trying to make sure my children would never have to feel what I felt growing up. I wanted them to feel emotionally safe, supported, nurtured.

And I've done that.

But the truth is, I've been so focused on protecting them that I forgot to protect myself.

I've worked so hard to give my children the emotional stability I never had. But in doing so, I've pushed myself past the point of exhaustion—over and over again. I tried to make our home a calm, loving space. I tried to meet every need, anticipate every mood, and prevent every storm.

And somewhere along the way, I forgot that I was allowed to have needs too.

I had become my own prison guard, cold and uncaring, relentlessly pushing myself for everyone else's sake.

I had forgotten about the little girl inside—small, frightened and alone—feeling as if her needs were too much.

A wave of compassion and desire to nurture washed over me as the realization hit me that I could care for her too.

Music had always been a way for me to process life, but as I started to realize, I would need much more than that. I realized that yoga may be necessary for me to learn how to connect back to myself and heal.

The phrase "mind-body connection" has been thrown around so much and yet I had never really given it much thought. There have been quite a few studies looking at the gut-brain connection through the lens of the trillions of bacteria living within. While we don't know everything yet, these studies have proven that there is a connection and further investigations will hopefully bring fascinating and therapeutic knowledge.

There is ample evidence to prove how our mental health can affect our physical health. While doctors will discuss how stress and anxiety can damage our bodies, healing that connection is rarely brought up. Exercise is always recommended but, in my experience, this doesn't necessarily address this connection.

Running, walking, strength training—all great for strengthening the body.

When I would engage in these exercises, I was never paying attention to my body.

In yoga, we must pay attention to our bodies, connecting movement with our breath and trying to relax certain muscles to allow for deeper stretching. Normally, I would move into a yoga pose, automatically engaging the needed muscles without thinking. Before this week, I had never tried to focus on specific muscles to make my body do something beyond its automatic response. The realization started to hit me that this was the key to bringing my mind and body back together again rather than having them be at war with each other.

I was beginning to understand the importance of mind-body-spirit connection in health and well-being. However, it can be easy for me to forget the importance of connection with others and how that can also impact well-being.

Little did I know that the universe would soon offer me lessons.

The Soundtrack of My Soul

That afternoon, we were on the road again—winding through the hills toward another avian rescue center in Tambor.

Thievery Corporation played from the van speakers—Latin-inspired electronica with touches of dub, bossa nova, and soul. It was a genre I didn't normally listen to back home, but the exotic sound fit the exotic landscape through which we drove.

I was reveling in the excitement of exploration—not knowing what would happen next. My childlike wonder was in full bloom.

I sat near Lindsay, and we started talking about music. Somewhere between songs, she mentioned that she loved the Woodstock era music.

My head swiveled. "Wait–you do?"

I told her I loved Jefferson Airplane and the Grateful Dead. She grinned and said she sings *Somebody to Love*.

Something inside me lit up–recognition of a like-minded soul. For once, I didn't have to explain my love for this music.

I fell in love with the music of the late '60s and early '70s when I was a young teenager. It resonated deeply–it was the soundtrack of my soul. My friends and family could not understand my music passion.

So, I'd learned to keep that part of myself hidden. It felt weird, out of place, a little too much for the world I lived in.

I listened in secret. I went to concerts I didn't care about just to fit in. I even tried to like country music during college because it was easier than being different.

But in that van, in that moment, something shifted.

I felt seen–for something that for others would seem small, but for me, it was huge.

I felt accepted, connected by music.

Though I had found people who would tolerate listening to my music, it was a rarity to meet someone who shared my passion. I felt myself building my tribe.

Before heading back, we stopped near Tambor Bay. Lindsay and I went in search of a bathroom, while the others went in search of cerveza.

Thank god Lindsay knew some Spanish. My grasp of the language was limited to, 'mi nombre es Sarah'—not helpful for rooting out a bathroom.

Luckily, we found one with ease. With bladders fully evacuated, we turned the corner to walk back to the van. The rest of the crew—successful in their mission—were walking towards us, passing beer to everyone. We fell into line with them and wandered over to the active beach area.

People were out either lounging or playing with each other—dogs intermingling as they ran around. We all sat together at a circular stone picnic table for a few minutes casually enjoying the warm beach air until Jeremy's phone rang. To give him privacy, Sonja, Sam and I decided to go walk, exploring the shoreline barefoot.

Past the sand, the shore was covered by water hyacinth, green ropes full of glossy leaves that felt cool under my feet. It was a welcome relief for the blisters that had formed on my heels.

The ocean of baby blue sky stretched endlessly above us with streaks of light gray clouds highlighted with brushstrokes of white. The shoreline below us gave me a sense of stability, dotted with little smooth stones of varying shades of brown and black. Under this magnificent sky, where the waters of Tambor Bay poured into Nicoya Bay, I lost all sense of existence outside of this moment in time. It was as if the soft lapping noises of the waves hitting the shore was lulling me into a hypnotic state.

I pulled out my phone to capture the beauty of this moment. Then, Sonja suggested taking a picture of me and Sam. We took turns taking pictures of each other in front of the picturesque Tambor Bay.

We could see the rest of the group heading back. It was getting late, but I was sad to leave. I wanted to stay—to explore this place slowly, quietly through my camera lens.

CHAPTER 23

The Mirror and the Critic

RETURNING TO THE CONDO, every inch of me dripping with sweat and my clothes drenched, I decided to shower and change. The feeling of fresh, dry clothes was a welcome relief. I pulled my hair up into a bun on top of my head and lay down, feeling relaxed.

With twenty minutes left before dinner, I decided to look through the pictures I'd taken in Tambor. I saw the photo of me and Sam on the beach.

My focus narrowed in on my body like that of a hawk searching for its prey. Through a very critical lens, I started to pick at all my bodily imperfections.

The inner critic started to say things like, "God, your arms look ginormous, fat and disgusting. You can see the rolls of fat down each side of your trunk. Your face is too broad, wrinkly and old looking. You aren't pretty anymore. You better crop that so that no one can see how fat your legs are."

As if to prove the critic right, I got off the bed to stare at myself in the mirror. Scanning from top to bottom, a look of disgust spread onto my face.

The critic continued relentlessly, "You look like you are stuffed into your clothes. Your legs are so short and squatty. You should be ashamed to go out looking like that."

With that, the tears welled up. The little girl inside couldn't handle the pain any longer. I decided that the critic was right. I shouldn't go out to dinner looking like this.

And so I didn't go to dinner. I couldn't. There was no coming out of that shame spiral once it started. Normally, it would take hours for me to calm down enough to quiet that voice–to gain control of my mind.

In a fit of rage, anger and self-hatred, I told Sam, through tears and with a firm and bitter voice, "I am not going to dinner tonight. You will have to go alone."

"No, I'll stay here with you," he said adamantly.

"I don't want you here. I want to be alone," I yelled at him.

"But I don't want to leave you like this. I'll go ask if we can get our dinners in here," he said, refusing to leave my side.

This only instilled more anxiety and agitation, "No, I don't want them to think that we're uppity and don't want to dine with them," referring to Sonja, Lindsay, and Tammy.

"I don't think any of them are going to think badly of you for not wanting to eat dinner with them right now," he placated.

"Can you just go get my dinner and bring it in here for me and then leave me alone and go eat with them? Please, I'm begging you," I said with a tone of finality.

Sam relented and walked over to the front door looking back at me one final time before closing the door. I lay back down on the bed with my head in my hands crying softly as another voice in my head spoke to me, "You are going to sound like a crazy person. Everyone will think so."

From there, it was like watching a rapid-fire tennis match as I listened to all the degrading comments flying around in my head. I was getting lightheaded.

A few minutes later, Sam walked in carrying a plate and some silverware as he spoke, "Are you sure you want me to eat dinner out there?" he asked.

By then, I had stopped crying and had calmed down some, replying, "I just want to be by myself."

He turned to leave, closing the sliding glass door behind him, leaving me to the cacophony of voices. I looked down at the plate full of rice, cooked vegetables and fresh shrimp. Every meal had been not only delicious, but healthy. Full of fresh meat or fish, vegetables and fruits, the meals were made with whole foods to nourish our bodies and minds. The fish or seafood was more robust in flavor than I'd ever tasted.

Yet, tonight, I had no desire to eat. In fact, I could still hear the voice telling me that I didn't deserve to eat dinner. This is not new. That particular voice loves to pop up and tell me that I don't deserve to eat something or drink something. It thinks that only thin people deserve to eat.

I could feel my logical mind try to take over. I know that all animals need to eat to survive. Even plants need to take in water and sunlight to make food for themselves. However, this abusive voice had long ago decided I don't deserve to eat because of the way I look.

That's when another voice, foreign in its cadence and language, surged to the foreground, "Eat the delicious and nutritious food."

I could hear the inner child respond, "I don't want to. I don't deserve to."

"Eat the nutritious food," it kept saying.

"I am too fat and shouldn't eat it so I can become fatter," the little voice argued back.

"Eat the nutritious food," it kept repeating.

The smaller voice quieted finally. Like a child who is upset over having to eat her veggies before she can leave the dinner table, I speared a piece of broccoli with my fork and very slowly, deliberately put it in my mouth.

I didn't savor the food. I ate because the voice told me to. Unlike the other meals, I didn't taste much of this meal. And I certainly didn't enjoy it. I picked out and ate only the shrimp and most of the veggies, leaving the rice to one side. Slowly, I ate half of the meal before moving the plate away from me.

The critical voices never came back, nor did the other voice telling me to eat the food. I thought about the message. Feeding ourselves is a way of nurturing our bodies as well as our minds and spirits. I had been raised to believe that eating was the way to get fat and to get criticized for my appearance.

Growing up, I would get constant lectures from my grandmother about how much a person should weigh for her height. She believed that a woman standing five feet tall should weigh no more than one hundred pounds. For every inch over five feet, one should add five pounds.

I have a muscular build like my father. I was never able to achieve HER goal for my height, one hundred and fifteen pounds. At my lowest weight, I was one hundred and twenty-seven pounds and a size four. I achieved that through self-castigation and by starving myself.

My grandmother placed the utmost importance on appearance, including body weight, looks and a sense of style. She always put her makeup on and dressed up even if she were only going to the grocery store. When asked, she said she did so because she never knew who she would see when out running errands. I learned that what other people thought of me, based on my appearance, was vastly more important than what I thought of myself. My coping mechanism was to make sure that I always weighed as little as I could, wore makeup and did my hair when leaving the house. And, I always wore clothing that accentuated my positive features and hid my bad features.

The Dean Martin song, *You're Nobody Until Somebody Loves You,* hit hard. This line was the mantra I was taught. I was taught that no one wants a fat, squatty, introverted, ugly, blob of a person and that is exactly how I saw myself from the time I was nine years old.

I had a brief reprieve in my late twenties and early thirties where I did feel good about my looks, but it was because I had finally molded myself into what my grandmother expected. I was dating or married throughout that time which only proved to me that she was right.

However, as I've had children and entered perimenopause, my body has betrayed me, or so the voices tell me. I'm larger than I've ever been in my life and am classified as obese. I'm not allowed to like myself and my body looking like this.

Though I have had decades of therapy and read many body positive articles and posts to know that I have to be kind to myself, true self-grace eludes me.

My body has produced three beautiful children, allowed me to feed them when they were infants and given me the strength to work in a physically demanding profession. I know I should be grateful, but I don't feel that.

When I look at other people, I don't judge them on their appearance. So, why do I continue to fight myself and my body? These fights have left me feeling drained, sad and isolated.

I didn't eat with my new friends that night because I felt ashamed, both of my body and of my downward spiral. I didn't want them to see me at my worst. Perhaps, at some level, I was worried that they would reject me, though my intuition told me that they would not have done so.

I was physically drained at that point, as these episodes usually leave me, and I wanted to change into pajamas and get under the blankets. I soothed my mind by numbing myself out with card games on my phone before letting my mind go offline for the day.

CHAPTER 24

The Calm After the Storm

Wednesday, December 11: *Waking to the sounds of the howler monkeys, I felt them beckoning me to come outside for the day. Grabbing my journal on my way out, I started to think about the night before.*

I hadn't experienced a shame spiral of that magnitude in a while. I realized that I don't have the energy or resources to combat either the triggers or their effects.

I was at a great crossroads in my life. I sat paralyzed, not knowing what to do. The same old patterns were holding me hostage. As if blindfolded, I could not see any other path but the one I'd been traveling. But I knew that I couldn't continue this way.

At the same time, I recognized that I had not once thought of work since arriving in Costa Rica. I could visualize the foundation of boundaries that I've started to build—not just for protection, but for thriving. Work had tried to force its way to me, trying to transport me from the jungle back to Kansas City. I stood firm and stayed in the present moment.

According to Eckart Tolle, the present moment is all we ever have. People say anxiety is living in the future and depression is living in the past. There is truth to this generalization. We can't act in the past or the future.

I think being a stranger in a foreign land with new, exotic experiences has grabbed my attention so fully—there is no room to allow my mind to wander to the past or future. I wondered how I could bring this presence back with me—into my real life.

As the sun rose, bringing her warmth, I remembered our 'homework' for the day—to set intentions for releasing habits and behaviors that no longer serve us. This exercise would become important later in the day.

Reflecting upon my ability to stay present, I realized I needed to stop allowing my self-worth to be dictated by how much I could do for others—or how industrious I appeared.

After last night, I no longer wanted to believe that my external appearance mandates my worth and beauty as a human.

I wanted to believe that love is my birthright, not something to earn.

Though I've worked diligently with my therapist to heal my inner child, I find it frustrating that healing isn't linear. Some days, I feel so proud to have come so far in my healing. Yet other days, it feels like I've only just embarked on this journey.

Last night was one of those days—the emotional pain and exhaustion overwhelming me. The need to distance myself from the rhetoric of my youth became more evident.

Perhaps the nearly 3062 miles that I traveled here from home had created the distance I needed to fully see my life—removing the heavily filtered lens I'd been carrying. It was becoming harder to feel compassion for the creators of that lens. I could see more boundaries that needed to be built so that I can thrive.

It was getting late. I closed my journal and went inside. I was more tired this morning as I walked over to the yoga platform, but I needed to go. I liked how I felt afterwards—tired, but refreshed.

CHAPTER 25

Tapped by Compassion

LINEA WAS DIFFERENT FROM any other yoga instructor I'd had. Her presence—and her uncanny ability to know exactly what we needed—was like a soothing balm on a raw wound. While I could feel strength building in my muscles and my flexibility growing, these sessions seemed to have an even greater effect on my overall sense of self.

Sitting on our mats, calming our minds and gently moving our bodies, Linea started the music. Her choice in music was, as usual, on par with its simple guitar strumming. The singer, her voice dark and weighted in lower tones, started the verse. As the chorus began, her voice became softer and more angelic as she ascended up an octave.

As the chorus continued, we moved into pigeon pose. We sat with our right leg bent, knee facing the right hand, while the left leg extended straight back. As the song crescendoed, we folded over the bent leg, laying our foreheads on our mats. Over and over again, the singer sang "remember why you came here, remember this life is sacred".

Linea softly spoke, "We all want to feel like we are cute all the time. It feels good, but our bodies change. Our worth is not wrapped up in what we look like. We are all beautiful souls. Our beauty shines from within, not from the outside. Every one of you is a beautiful soul."

As we sat in this pose, meant to release emotional blockages, tears silently started to well up within my lower lid threatening to pour over the side at any minute. There was no sobbing, only tears that eventually freed themselves from the confines of my eyelids, rolling down in a single line.

Linea's message, after last night's episode of self-reproach, had overwhelmed me with validation and loving compassion. It was almost too much to process. Her words—a contradiction to the angry critic's message from last night—enveloped me. Sadness, heartbreak and gratitude flowed from me in response to her simple yet beautiful message.

I tried to recover quickly—to conceal my tears as we moved into the next series of poses. I refocused my attention to my body and my breath, short and erratic as it was, to calm my body and mind.

After class, I started putting the mats away in the wooden closet, fighting with the rickety sliding doors. Sonja and Linea were talking quietly as I overheard Linea tell Sonja that this was a judgement-free zone.

I couldn't bear it any longer. I had no energy left to stop my emotions. Grief, sadness, and anger rose like a tide, along with a desperate longing for the pain to end. I didn't have the strength to suppress it anymore.

Hearing me cry, Linea and Sonja both rushed to my side. "I've never experienced a judgement-free zone," I said, sobbing. Like the perfect student I was, I had learned to be a particularly acerbic self-critic. With this maddening roommate, I could never escape criticism.

Without hesitation, Linea took my wrist in her lithe hands, placing the pads of her fingers on my wrist as if she were taking my pulse.

"Think of a time when you were shown love," she whispered.

I thought of my youngest daughter. Not long ago, I was sick with a bad cold. She would not leave my side. She escorted me to the bathroom, brought me water and Kleenex and lay beside me, rubbing my back to help me sleep. Sad to see me sick, she just wanted to make me feel better.

Linea asked, "Can I tap on your face?"

"Yes," I responded, knowing exactly what she was doing.

She started tapping above my eyebrow using her middle and forefinger as she spoke, "You are loved. You are worthy of love. You are a beautiful soul who is loved by so many." She repeated this message as she moved to my temple, then my upper lip and chin, finishing up along my collarbone. She repeated this several times. Typically, tapping is used to validate negative emotions, process and then release them as you install more positive beliefs.

Within a few minutes, my heart had stopped racing, my breath normalizing. My grief had emptied itself out.

Later, I told Sam that I wished I could have left my body to watch this experience. This spectacular display of intuition, compassion and human healing was nothing short of breathtaking.

Humans have boundless abilities to heal ourselves and others. To do so, we must be connected. I had lost that connection.

I used to love talking to and being around people. I thought of myself as a people person. I enjoyed going to parties and events surrounded by people.

As I've gotten older, these settings have started to induce

anxiety. I prefer being at home with my kids without anything to do. I crave the peace and safety that comes to me the second I step into my home.

My therapist told me that social anxiety is common amongst people who grew up with judgement and criticism. Assuming that if their families, those who were supposed to love them the most, were this critical, then the rest of the world must be so too.

Suddenly, this revelation made sense. Like Sherlock Holmes having just solved a case—it's elementary.

It's hard to find the connection and compassion that I grew up craving when I am scared to venture out into the world exposed, raw. Here, I had met complete strangers and in just three days, been shown nothing but deep connection and compassion without hesitation. Trusting that truth felt daunting.

CHAPTER 26

My Venn Diagram

THAT MORNING, WE DISCUSSED the stages of burnout. Burnout often begins with the belief that you have to prove yourself.

I have always looked young for my age. In the early stages of my career, I would walk into exam rooms having to prove that I was the doctor. Most people assumed I was a young tech. Some even asked me, even after I did my exam, when the veterinarian was going to step into the room.

Imposter syndrome only exacerbated the feeling of having to prove that I was capable to my clients, my bosses and my colleagues.

With each positive experience that I had at work, I would get a rush of endorphins. It eased the ache left from not feeling like I was enough—good enough, smart enough, caring enough. Like an addict needing another hit, I learned to push myself more for the validation I received.

As I worked harder and did more for my clients, the high that I got fooled me into thinking I could outrun the imposter. Throughout the years, the imposter would make an appearance and then disappear for longer stretches—my experience fueling my confidence.

I failed to see that I had trained myself to regularly put the needs of my employers and clients above my own needs. So dependent upon external validation, I worked longer hours, ignoring my own needs—sleep, time with my family, and down time. This self-denial was so insidious that I failed to see the issue.

Resentment had started to nest within. I had started to blame the entire veterinary profession, assuming that everyone trained their clients to expect full access all the time.

The lines had become blurred between me and my clients. When dealing with volatile situations—becoming the scapegoat for clients' grief and anger—I assumed the guilt. Complaints about the cost of my services arose, despite all my efforts to keep pricing as low as possible, and I accepted the shame. I felt out of control as if the system had been rigged all along.

I had also become cynical. I tried desperately to hide from all humans when not working.

Panic met me as soon as I opened my eyes each workday morning. Taking Xanax and doing tapping sessions were part of my morning ritual before leaving the house.

Leaving my children—my emotional safety—left me feeling terror-stricken like I was walking into a war zone.

Trepidation often started on Sunday mornings as I dreaded going to sleep at night knowing that the next morning, I would have to step back into the battle zone. I told myself the day wouldn't kill me—but some mornings, hauling a horse trailer through a city full of aggressive drivers, I wasn't so sure.

I had found despair nesting in its dark pit.

I became paralyzed with fear and shame. I could see no viable path forward at this point.

When Sonja pulled up the power point slide showing the bell curve to explain each stage of burnout, my eyes slid over to the far right to see the symptoms of end-stage burnout. Recognition hit me like a freight train—flattening me.

As shame and fear washed over me—tears flooded my eyes and my body started to shake.

As if connected by some invisible thread, Sonja halted the session as she looked at me. Lindsay turned to me and immediately threw her arms around me in a big bear hug. It was one of those hugs that tells you that you're safe. Resting my head on her shoulder, I let go. In doing so, my awareness came back to the sound of Lindsay's heartbeat.

"Your heart is beating so fast," I told her. "I'm sorry if this is triggering to you."

"Stop it. I'm fine and so are you," Lindsay said holding me tightly.

As she released her grip, Tammy had found what she was searching for in her bag and slid a tablet down towards me.

"Xanax…pass it down to Sarah," Tammy said.

Lindsay grabbed my water cup and pushed it in my direction, "Take it. Here's your water," she said gently.

Both Lindsay and Tammy had admitted to hitting their rock-bottom, end-stage burnout last year. Both, in separate instances, had mentioned that they were nervous about being triggered and slipping backwards. I was acutely aware of not wanting to push them away with my emotions. I tried to quickly soothe myself further until the Xanax had time to sink in.

During our mid-session break, I reluctantly walked back to the condo where I'd left Sam. That morning, we'd argued again. He had been emotionally distant for many years. I had been trying to get him to see the disconnection in our relationship and help mend it.

Taking any conversation from me as an accusation, he had become defensive and withdrew even more. It felt like we were stuck in the movie *Groundhog Day*—each day an exact replica of the last.

If I thought we had finally understood each other, a few days later, we'd have the same argument all over again.

I had sunk into despair not only about my work, the world we lived in, but also about my marriage and our ability to seek connection ever again. I truly thought I was bringing up constructive criticism only to be met with blame and defensiveness stemming from his insistence that he was a victim.

Walking into our room, I was apprehensive. I was way too emotionally frail to have an argument and open old wounds. The Xanax had started to affect me—my muscles felt like they were made of gelatin. Though tired and relaxed, I knew that it wouldn't take much provocation to spur my anger and frustration.

I took my time in the bathroom, avoiding any confrontations. Running out of time before the next session, I came back out to where Sam was to grab a diet Pepsi—much needed caffeine to keep me awake.

"I want to tell," Sam tentatively started to say.

"No," I said, holding up my palms to him in a halting manner. "I can't do this anymore. I need to make it through the rest of this morning's session and I've already gotten so emotional that Tammy had to get me Xanax. So, I just can't keep doing this anymore."

"No, no, I wanted to tell you that you were right. I stayed in here and have been watching you tube videos on rejection sensitivity and rejection sensitive dysphoria and it all makes sense. It is exactly what I think. I think that you are rejecting me, even when you aren't. Then, I get angry or start to retreat. You are right. I am going to go back to my doctor and ask for help with this," he said in a rush to get it out before I could stop him.

I slowly dropped my hands, relaxing my shoulders and back, only then becoming aware that I was bracing my body for a fight.

Apprehensive about trusting this admission, I kept my distance emotionally. "That's good. I'm glad you found something that has helped shed some light on how your mind works. I have got to get back to the platform to start the rest of the lecture," I gently replied.

"Go," he said, a barely perceptible smile forming, "I'm going to keep watching more videos."

We finished for the day discussing ways to decrease our mental load, learning how to compartmentalize tasks. For me, my mind was constantly humming. I used to think of the separation of work and home life as putting on different hats. Like Mr. Rogers putting on his cardigan and changing shoes when he walked in the door, I put my veterinary hat on the second I walked into work. Under that hat, it was as if my personal life did not exist. For the most part, it worked in reverse as well. During the weekends, I could forget that I was a veterinarian. At home, I was a wife and a mother.

Somewhere along the way, that separation was smudged out. Starting my own clinic completely overwhelmed me with worry and responsibility. My life was like a Venn diagram—each role I played represented by a circle. But, in my diagram, all of the circles sat on top of one another—looking like it was just one circle.

My mind was tired. I couldn't even begin to think about strategies for improvement at this point. It wasn't even noon and it felt like I had been on an emotional rollercoaster all day.

CHAPTER 27

The Communion of All Life

AT LUNCH THAT DAY, the conversation was light with frequent laughter. The group sensed that we needed a break from heavier feelings.

Everyone retreated to their rooms except for Sonja and me. Galina was on the phone a few feet away. As we languished under the canopy, we were visited by an iguana who had lost half of his tail, leaving just a short stub. He walked towards our dining table pausing to look at us with curiosity. He sat there motionless for several minutes before running past us.

Within seconds, I saw something move in my periphery—a gorgeous turquoise iguana who had walked into our area like a mighty warrior. He paused in almost the same exact spot where the other iguana had previously stood, watching us. He then started to bounce his head up and down as if enjoying the beat of good song.

"Aww, cute little guy," Sonja remarked, "that's a very territorial move right there."

"The head bouncing movement?" I questioned, turning to her.

"Yes," she responded. "it's probably why the other iguana ran away. And it may be how he lost his tail."

"Ooooh, that makes sense," I said, looking back to the other iguana who was clearly scared.

But, then I noticed that the turquoise one was walking over to me. With his beady little eyes focused on me, he inched closer and closer.

"He knows I'm not an iguana, right?" I asked, nervously.

"You should sit down and stay still," Sonja whispered.

This didn't inspire confidence in me. I slowly sat down, not taking my eyes off the iguana. He stopped within three feet of my chair and stared me down. Bobbing up and down in front of me, he was showing me that he was the boss here.

It felt like an eternity, but he finally walked off looking like John Wayne, following the first iguana.

It was thrilling to be so close to these wild creatures. A rush of gratitude swept over me as I thought of how privileged I was to get to be immersed in this animal kingdom.

As humans, we think we rule the world, but this experience taught me that we don't. We are simply a small part of an entirely interconnected array of life. This was not a zoo, nor were these animals trained. They were telling us what their rules were and if we were smart, we listened–respecting their way of life. Peace reigned in this situation because of my attention to, and respect for, the iguana–I was the stranger here. But, it was easy to feel like a part of nature here. This connection with the natural world–something far larger than myself–was strangely comforting. This sense of belonging was something that I have never felt before.

Growing up, I felt like an outsider, a stranger even within my own family. I tried desperately to fit in, to belong. The older I got, the harder I tried to fit in. I desperately tried to be the right size and weight. The makeup, the hair, the way I spoke and acted—all to show the world that I was a properly educated girl with manners who knew her place.

However, that little box—the one in which I was stuffed—was getting unbearably snug. The longer I stayed trapped inside, the more painful it was.

My spirit was trying desperately to grow, to move past the restrictions. Rather than break down the barriers of that box, I slowly started to kill off parts of me to stay confined in the box.

Not until my late 40's did I start to wear clothes that highlighted my true sense of style, to wear my hair in a messy bun on top of my head, to stop wearing makeup every time I left the house. Initially, this felt like blasphemy, but slowly it started to feel more natural.

I started to feel more natural.

Because I followed such rigid rules around my appearance for so long, I still struggle to breathe through my diaphragm—pushing my belly out as I inhale. I was trained to suck my belly in, to appear thinner.

Letting go of that will take time. So will letting go of the fear of judgement.

But, here, in this place where every living thing has a place, I felt at home. I felt comforted and nurtured in a way I have never felt or known.

The biophilia hypothesis comes from the idea that humans have an innate desire to connect with nature. It is this interconnectedness that makes us feel like we are a part of a larger ecosystem rather than believing that we are separate.

This deep sense of attachment to all other living things is more palpable here in the jungle. The sounds, smells and sights all help to bring me profound comfort as I discover how to heal in a way that is sustainable. The jungle has been like a loving and wise mother who intuitively knows what her daughter needs, ever ready to provide.

For a brief moment, as the iguana shared his space with me, I felt a peace I've never before felt. Just then, the illusion of separateness fell away showing the communion of all life.

When we feel disconnected with all living things, we tend to feel like we need to defend or protect ourselves—our egos. Ironic that it was the iguana's show of dominance and need to defend his territory that allowed me to recognize my unity with nature.

CHAPTER 28

Breathing Into Myself

THAT AFTERNOON, WE HEADED to Montezuma for a sound healing session. Having done a few of these, I was excited for the chance to relax and do nothing. After parking the car, we had a short hike along the beach to get to the practitioner's house. To my right, the turquoise waters and their white caps hit the rocks gently on the rocky shore creating a soft shushing noise. To my left, the jungle crept in close as if it wanted to listen to the water's sound.

We continued to walk along the shore before finding an inconspicuous sandy path that crept behind the palm trees. Like follow the leader, we were led in single file up to a small wooden bridge-like structure where we were told to take off our shoes.

The thatched roof stone structure in front of us welcomed us through its open front door. I followed the rest of the group up the tile stairs that opened up to a large open-air bedroom. There were no walls except for the one that held the bed's headboard. There were two large hardwood posts in the opposite corners of the room along which the sheer curtains hung, blowing in the light breeze.

It was a large room and at least ten to fifteen others were milling about getting themselves ready. Galina walked by and told us to pick up a yoga mat and a blanket from the corner near the bed. I followed Pam across to the other side of the room closest to the beach where the clouds and palm leaves filtered the sun's rays.

The feeling of the delicate breeze and the sound of the soft, rhythmic waves on the rocky beach gave me a sense of what returning to heaven or source might be like.

The teacher asked us to lie down on our mats, using our blankets as a head rest, and relax.

My first sound healing session was almost a year ago. The practitioner had started with a short explanation of the theories behind sound healing. I had found it fascinating. She had explained how we are all made up of atoms that vibrate at different rates or frequencies. Sound is also made up of different vibrations. Those vibrations can affect the atoms that are our building blocks.

She then showed us images of water molecules and the shapes created when exposed to different sounds. These images were taken from Dr. Masaru Emoto's book, *The Hidden Messages in Water*. In it, he explains his experiment where he exposed water to both positive and negative words. The results were staggering. When positive words were spoken, the water formed beautiful and highly organized patterns. However, when negative words were spoken, the water was disorganized and rather unpleasant in appearance. Since our bodies are made up of about 60 percent water and our brains are about 75 percent water, we can draw astonishing conclusions about how sound affects our bodies.

This has also been shown in studies done in classrooms across the country where kids speak kindly to one plant and bully another. The results all show similar effects. Plants that were spoken to kindly all thrived, whereas the other plants did not.

While most of us would assume that we all do better when we

are shown kindness rather than hatred, I had not thought of sound as being a healing tool. During my first two experiences with sound healing, I had been able to feel my body relax as though I was having a full body massage. It had been difficult to rouse myself after the first session. I just wanted to drift off to sleep afterwards. So, I was eager to get started with this session.

From the seminars this week, I had learned several things about myself. The first being that I have a neurotic personality type. I previously thought the word was merely a synonym for psychotic or crazy. However, it is one of the big five personality traits. It refers to someone who has more tendencies towards anxiety, self-doubt, depression, worry or emotional distress.

Learning that veterinarians are significantly more likely to be neurotic versus the general population, I was not alone. Neurotic personality types are more likely than others to experience burnout, which made sense, sadly.

Ironically, as I thought about the blurred boundaries and loss of self, certain truths became clearer. Without boundaries, I was headed for certain self-destruction. I was a people-pleasing, overachieving, neurotic empath—a dumpster fire on wheels.

I was ready to close my eyes and open myself to whatever experience was going to unfold, knowing that it could do nothing but help at this point.

As I lay there, the warm and humid breeze swirling about me, I closed my eyes as the therapist started using her instruments.

The initial clang of the Tibetan bowl turned into a softer reverberation, weakening as time went on. This acted as the off button to my consciousness.

Despite clouds blocking most of the sun, I could suddenly see a bright light beyond my closed eyelids as if the sun were directly over my head. I could see, as if my eyes were not closed at all, that I was on a bright white patio basking under the brilliant ocean blue sky, feeling the heat radiate from overhead.

Lying there, I felt the sun taking stress and tension from my body while replenishing it with peace, joy and stillness. It was a cycle of taking and giving simultaneously.

As time passed, my body felt heavier, melting into the floor beneath me. Eventually, I no longer felt as if I was tethered to my body.

At that point, I could see, behind my closed eyelids, an expansive ocean of azure blue and feel myself swimming with other creatures of the sea, without the need for air. The freedom I felt was like nothing I had experienced before. There was no time, no bodily constraints, no past or future. I was fully experiencing the present moment with no thoughts or expectations of what was going to happen next. As if watching a movie in my mind, I could feel the warmth on my skin and the gentle breezes coming off the bay not 15 yards from where I was.

I lay basking in pure bliss for what seemed like hours until the teacher started to speak, alerting us to the fact that the sound healing session had ended.

We sat up, keeping our eyes closed, as she sealed the practice with words of gratitude and respect for our time together. We bowed our heads and spoke the word namaste, meaning the spirit within me honors and recognizes the spirit within you. This word helps create a sacred connection between people by recognizing that we are all filled with the same spirit.

Though I interact with people all day every day, these interactions were often more superficial, not the deeply fulfilling connections that my soul craved.

As an introvert, social interactions were draining, even when they were positive. Thus, I had learned that I needed to take my weekends to recharge my batteries. I rarely left my house on Saturdays and Sundays. I found that spending time with my children, not worrying about what others thought of me, allowed me to fully relax.

However, I was starting to feel the isolation wear on me. Feeling connected during this class had not drained me. It allowed me to see that not every social situation required something from me other than to be myself.

I didn't always have to be something for someone else.

This thought flies in the face of what I was raised to believe. I, much like many women, was taught from a tiny age that my worth was found in what I could do for others. Love was achieved, not just given freely. I had learned that love was primarily based on physical attributes. If you were not given the most beautiful features, you then had to rely upon what you could do for someone else to obtain love and attention. Furthermore, I wasn't allowed to feel good about myself without another person's attraction to me.

I could force myself to be outgoing during work, but I shied away from most social interactions for fear of being maligned. The people in this room were not casting aspersions. In fact, I felt so utterly *un*-judged since touching down in Costa Rica. I had only just noticed that I could breathe into being fully me without any hesitation or fear.

The difference here was stark.

Back home, it felt like all the air was being sucked out of the room. Here, there was this expansive and loving energy in which to bask. It was as though I could feel myself getting lighter.

As we walked outside and stopped to put our shoes on, Galina looked at her watch and said, "Oh shoot. I didn't realize how late it is. We should have been at Letitia's a while ago. We need to hurry up."

CHAPTER 29

A Moonlit Conversation with the Universe

THE DAY BEFORE, GALINA had told us about Horse Spirit Healing. Immediately recognizing the name, I quickly told the group how we had flown to Cobano with the owner's mother. As she explained horse spirit meditation, all of us were excited to have that experience. As it happened, the only time we had available was also the only time Letitia had availability.

It was kismet.

We walked quickly away from the beach to the parking lot. Piling into the large Suburban, we drove fifteen minutes or so back through Montezuma. Stopping on a little mud driveway, we could see the gates of the horse sanctuary. Not knowing what to expect, I was a little apprehensive about this experience. But, I have always loved horses and I was excited for whatever came next. To the right, there was a quaint house with a concrete covered patio. Letitia, a petite woman with long blonde wavy hair, called out from the pasture beyond the drive welcoming us to the sanctuary as she walked toward us.

She invited us to take our shoes off and come sit at the hardwood table on the patio. After the introductions, we signed our waivers before heading over to the pasture with the horses.

As we walked, she explained that we would be interacting with the herd in an entirely different way than we were likely taught. Instead of walking up to the horses and immediately raising our hands to pet them, we were to slowly walk towards them without touching them. Disappointment crept up—I was so excited to nuzzle with a horse.

Letitia led us over to a tree just outside of the gated pasture to a circle of plastic chairs. She invited us to pick up a stone that had words written on them. Then, we went around and told the group our words and what they meant to us. The word focus was written on mine in red ink.

"Focus. I think it's telling me to pay attention to what my mind is focused on." I said, with some uncertainty as if there was a right and wrong answer.

Dusk had arrived as we finished going around the circle. After the last person spoke, Letitia started telling us about her herd. Almost every single horse had been rescued from a traumatic situation, hence the sanctuary.

"All the horses here, except one, have histories of trauma from humans. That horse was born to one of the mares here at the sanctuary," she explained in a soothing, hypnotic voice. She went on to explain how horses are love and joy in physical form. "Together they are grounded in this place and with each other. Being in their presence can bring healing to anyone," she went on.

At my core, I love animals and want to connect with them all. So, this new way of being present with them without physical contact was such a foreign concept. I wondered if it felt strange to anyone else.

We listened as Letitia held up a pictorial view of the chakras, or energy centers, of the horse explaining their locations, comparing them with the human locations.

She explained in a hushed tone, "When you enter the pasture, just walk slowly towards the horse that you feel drawn to. Go slowly and just remember not to walk up and touch the horse."

I entered the pasture feeling quite a bit more anticipation and nervousness than I expected. A sense of not wanting to do the wrong thing laid heavy on my shoulders.

Though there was still a little light, darkness would soon be upon us. The moon was out, but not yet brilliant.

Just twenty or so feet away, there were two horses, a paint and a roan colored horse standing very close to one another. As she walked among us, Letitia introduced each horse by name, sharing a little about his or her story.

When she got closer to where I was standing, she said in her soft, soothing voice, "Then, there's Mahala, the paint horse and next to her is BeLoved. She had been severely traumatized in her life before the sanctuary. She gives us the gift of unconditional worthiness and presence."

As she went on to talk about the rest of the herd, I stayed focused on Mahala, who was closer to me than any of the others by only a few feet. However, my attention was being pulled towards BeLoved. I was struck by the similarities between the two of us.

Having grown up feeling like I was a burden, I never wanted anyone else to feel like that. I tried to ensure that everyone had my rapt attention so that they would never feel the way I often felt— unworthy of attention.

Mahala started to move towards the back of the pasture slowly but steadily. BeLoved stayed where she was as I continued stepping closer to her. For ten minutes or so, she stood there with her rear haunches facing me. Periodically, she would turn her head to look back towards me and then return her attention to something out in front of her.

I had walked to within fifteen feet of her, stopping short not wanting to spook her. I was unsure of how close we were supposed to be. Letitia had told us we'd be able to feel their healing energy.

I remembered Letitia's instruction—to set the intention for what we needed from this experience. I didn't know exactly what I needed—I only knew I came here to heal from burnout.

BeLoved turned to her left and slowly plodded towards a large water tank. By that time, Pam, another veterinarian in our group, had redirected her attention towards us. Now, Pam and I stood on either side of the beautiful roan mare. BeLoved stood frozen for ten minutes before she, and soon Pam, began to retreat to the back of the pasture.

By now, it was dark and the moon, directly overhead, spread a soft silvery white light over the pasture. There were some long thin clouds that streaked throughout the sky periodically covering the moon before moving onward.

Despite the moonlight, I couldn't see the others.

I was alone once more.

This awareness had incited an overwhelming sense of sadness and grief within me. With tears welling up and my legs too tired to hold me anymore, I slowly sank down to the dirt pasture beneath me.

As my gaze moved up to the moon, I felt panic wondering if this was my rock bottom. Here I was, sitting in a pasture surrounded by horse manure in rural Costa Rica, alone and crying.

With nothing to lose, I started to talk to the universe.

"I'm so tired of chasing love and of begging people to love me. I

can't even get a horse to pay me attention. What is so innately wrong with me that I am unworthy of such love and attention?"

My nose started to feel congested as it does when I cry, forcing me to breathe through my mouth. With nothing to wipe my face or nose, I sat tear soaked, unable to breathe easily.

I looked down at the dirt, realizing that I had made a decision. I was no longer going to chase anyone, begging for love and attention. I had stopped that a while ago with many in my life, save a few. The realization hit me that my way of moving through this world with the intention of achieving others' love and respect was no longer sustainable. Beneath that realization was a fear that this might leave me alone in this world with only my angry, harsh, critical internal roommate for company.

At that moment, I saw something move in the moonlight. It was ChiChi, Letitia's little dog. She had not paid a single bit of attention to me when we were sitting on her patio or under the tree by the pasture. ChiChi had wanted to sit in Pam's lap and with Sonja and Lindsay before that. I had made note that not even the dog had wanted to come to me beforehand.

Now, she was slowly trotting from the back of the pasture towards the front. She was about twenty or so feet away from me and facing away from me. Suddenly she looked to her left and immediately started running quickly right to me. Her tail was up and she crawled into my lap begging for belly rubs and love. It was almost as if the universe had heard my pain and decided to send me an answer in the form of this sweet little joyful creature.

The word chichi can refer to a nursemaid and in that moment, this little dog became a loving caretaker for me. Showering me in loving kisses, licking the tears from my face and asking for me to love on her, this little but mighty creature was able to overcome my enormous sense of fear and despair. In my anguish over being left behind once more to chase, I had been sent love. So focused on the horses walking away from me, I could easily have missed the love that ChiChi was trying to share in that moment.

I have spent decades of my life trying to get the people in my life to love me, often without success. But, had I been open to receiving love from others in my life during the process? I started to look at my life from a more objective lens—seeing that I had squandered so much time chasing love. While doing so, I had not registered any deep human connection from other sources.

There were probably thousands of moments within my lifetime where friends, teachers, clients and even strangers had shown me love and respect. But, since that message wasn't coming from those within my focus, it didn't carry as much weight. I had grown up internalizing the idea that I wasn't worthy, so I struggled to receive loving compassion from anyone else.

As this realization hit me, I could hear voices coming from the back of the pasture. Within minutes, the whole group was upon me as I stood, brushing off the dirt from my legs. I tried to wipe my tear-soaked cheeks, but the beauty of this lesson clung to me. With each blink, a fresh wave of tears filled my eyes threatening to run down my cheeks again. Thankfully, it was so dark that my eyes wouldn't reveal my current emotion to the rest of the group. Only Letitia stopped me as the rest headed towards Sam and Galina, who had decided to have a beer at the local dive down the road instead.

"I didn't see you at the back of the pasture, I wondered where you were," Letitia innocently said.

At that moment, I knew my voice, thin and reedy, would betray me as it came out strained against the rising tears, "I just gave up. I am so tired of chasing people and things begging to be loved. I just don't have the energy to chase anymore."

"I want this one back," Letitia told Galina as she grabbed hold of me in a big momma bear hug. "You have to let me have her back."

She continued to hold me in her clutches as she cooed to me like I was her infant, "Oh baby girl, sweet baby girl, the horses were trying to lead you back to the rest of the herd in the back of the pasture. They weren't walking away from you. They were leading you."

"No," I tried telling her, "I actually had the experience I needed tonight and I'm so grateful. ChiChi came over to me and sat with me, loving on me."

I relaxed in her grip some more before speaking again, "I used the time to speak to the universe and ChiChi was its response."

"You come back again and let the herd help you," she said once more as she loosened her arms, cooing once more.

That was the hard part–letting someone help me.

CHAPTER 30

The Threads that Shaped My Life

THE RIDE BACK TO the facility was short, but it was enough time to control my breathing and stop the tears. I listened to the happy sounds of the rest of my group talk about their experiences while I stayed silent. The rest of the evening was uneventful as we enjoyed yet another simple and elegant meal under the vast expanse of stars and twinkle lights on the canopy. I had finally gotten used to the heat and humidity and found it to be a thoroughly pleasant evening to be sitting outside, as close to idyllic as one could expect. As I lay in the cool white sheets that night, I could see the threads that had shaped my life into a self-defeating, isolating cycle.

CHAPTER 31

The Promise of a Better Story

Thursday, December 12: *I arose at my new normal time–5:30am. I quietly slipped out through the sliding glass door to my spot on the deck. In anticipation of the sun's first peek above the horizon, I opened my journal to reflect upon and record the previous day's events.*

The magnitude of pain that I'd been carrying throughout my life hit me as if gravity was so much stronger here. I could no longer carry it.

Silently, I set an intention to leave all that I could here in the jungle. I was tired of crying. The onslaught of panic attacks had left me drained. I began to see them for what they were— messages from my body telling me to let go. I had to leave this pain—a combination of grief over the relationships I had hoped for and never had, the overwhelm of trying to meet grandiose expectations, and the fear of not being enough for my children and clients—behind.

This life was no longer sustainable for me.

For months, a single message had shown up on my phone almost daily, always in the afternoon, always the same:

"Don't be afraid to start all over again. You may like your new story better."

I took it as a sign–proof that something needed to change. And then, just as suddenly as it had appeared, it stopped.

That silence felt like a dare from the universe: Now it's your turn.

From day one, I believed it was the universe whispering that change was necessary. The promise of a better story was comforting, especially when I felt like I was living within a raging tempest. Back then, I couldn't see past the storm—not knowing how to get out.

In thinking of my new creation story, I must make more of an effort to move my body in a very intentional way. Waking early to do yoga this week at 6:30am has been a wonderful way to start the day. I would never have guessed this—I am not a morning person.

Here, my master clock quickly synchronized to the rhythm of the sun. It was as though the sun was beckoning me as she peaked over the oceanic horizon.

But beyond the effortlessness of waking so early, I felt even more energy here as though the jungle was offering it up with abundance. Others spoke about the magic of Costa Rica, but nothing could have prepared me for this.

I had found rejuvenation in the rainforest of the Nicoya Peninsula. Some believe that it is due to powerful vortexes here said to replenish the body, mind, and spirit. Though I didn't know much about vortexes, friends who had gone to those in Sedona recounted having profound experiences. They explained that there were places where energy is either spiraling into or out of the Earth.

Found all over the globe, these are physical locations where people go to become introspective and begin moving towards personal transformation and healing. I now understood what so many others have felt visiting Sedona. I could feel a potent release of the negative energy and rapid filling of the good. It was palpable.

As the sun rose higher, I had to close my journal for the morning to ready myself for yoga, then breakfast. After a beautifully colorful breakfast of waffles with assorted fresh fruit and tamarind juice, everyone was eager to start the morning's seminar.

We were supposed to have filled out a questionnaire earlier in the week, indicating how often the listed statements applied to us. It was a collection of experiences shared by people impacted by secondary traumatic stress or compassion fatigue–realities that affect most caretaking professions. Coming here, I already knew I had felt this. It was a source of shame. I never spoke of it because I didn't want anyone to think I was no longer capable of caring.

Because I still cared—a lot.

A lifetime of hearing and holding emotionally painful stories had left me overwhelmed and shut down, unable to take in anything more.

Moving down the list, I tallied up the points based on how frequently the statements were true for me. My total was 59. Anything over 49 indicated severe secondary traumatic stress. While this wasn't shocking, it still felt like a diagnosis I wasn't ready to hear.

The severity of my distress was still sinking in. Like going to the doctor about a tiny mole only to hear that you have a cancerous melanoma, it takes time to process the information and what that means for your future.

This scale had forced me to re-evaluate how I relate to the world. I'd thought of boundaries as a means of disconnection rather than seeing them as protection for myself.

I am an empath–I can feel the emotions of others as if they were my own. This has created confusion around what feelings were my own versus those of others'. Both my superpower and my kryptonite, my empathy has allowed me to be a compassionate caretaker and create deep connections with people. However, uncontrolled, it has led to higher stress, emotional overload, and the inability to set boundaries with people— placing others' needs above my own.

An empath without boundaries is headed for certain self-destruction.

As I absorbed all that Sonja had taught us, the cognizance that I would have to create changes quickly hit me. I would have to learn how and where to create such boundaries before I leave for home.

Whereas before, the idea of not being afraid of creating a new story was a gentle suggestion, now it was imperative.

CHAPTER 32

Reaching Through the Dark

THAT MORNING, WE SPOKE about self-care which would normally evoke a groan and an eye roll from me. Who has time for this? But now, it felt like an urgent need.

We were given homework–fill out another questionnaire broken up into several categories of self-care including physical, mental, emotional, work and social wellbeing. Briefly glancing at the statements, I realized that a lot of this was not time-consuming and could be integrated immediately. Hope surged.

A thought occurred to me as I read the line asking if I treated myself with kindness. I have a self-deprecating sense of humor and when I make mistakes, I tend to verbally call out my stupidity. Thinking back to the images of water while someone shouted out negative words, I realized how many times per day this happens. I needed to stop reprimanding myself immediately. This was attainable.

I looked through the rest of the list, noting other targets of change—breathing deeply, spending time outside, and making my goals a priority. This unlocked other ideas as well—limits at work, disengaging periodically, and delegating more to my technicians who are wanting to do more for me.

I could finally start to feel the upswing, both mentally and physically—a hand reaching down to me in my dark pit of despair.

That hand was my own.

CHAPTER 33

For the Love of Bittersweet Chocolate

LATER THAT AFTERNOON, WE were able to go on a chocolate tour at Indigena Chocolate, just a few minutes drive from where we were staying. We walked up the dirt path to the simple metal-roofed structure. It was surrounded by tall deep green foliage with fuchsia blossoms. Shorter palms dotted the path showing their emerald green leaves. A gentle breeze blew through, exposing their deep purple undersides. All of the plant beds were demarcated with rows of empty coke, wine and liquor bottles, their necks buried in the dirt. A thin veil of dust and dirt had settled onto their surfaces over the years. Like little glass soldiers, the bottles protected the plants from getting toppled by humans and animals alike.

The dirt path opened onto an outdoor patio with several long tables. Standing near the entrance was a tall, lean gentleman whose kind smile stood out above all else. Gianni, an Italian expat, was as gregarious as he was tall, exuberantly welcoming us to his café. He gestured for us to have a seat at a table of hard Costa Rican wood with various bowls and offerings already laid out.

As we walked past a small bush, the tiniest of bees swarming the bush, Sonja mentioned that these were Mariolas stingless bees. They are gentle and much smaller than many of the bee species in North America. They have been domesticated in many places—their honey medicinal.

I followed Sam to sit next to him. He sat down without a glance—claiming the space, leaving none for me. It felt purposeful—stinging me. I paused before walking back to the other side of the table finding a seat at the opposite end. To me, this represented how disconnected we were.

I felt suffocated—as if, in this open air space, there was not enough room to breathe. Holding back tears, I tried to observe without judgement.

Grateful for the distraction, Gianni came over carrying a sweet cake drizzled with honey. He explained that the honey came from the sweet little bees that we had walked past earlier. It was a heavy cake with just a touch of sweetness. I wanted to devour the rest of the cake, finding comfort in its sweetness, but I also knew there was more to come—and I didn't want to miss what came next.

Gianni then passed around plates of spoons already filled with chocolate. These were loaded with chocolate that was 67% cacao. We would follow that with chocolates that were 75 percent, 82 percent and 100 percent cacao. I knew the chocolate would become increasingly more bitter as the concentrations increased.

The 67 percent cacao struck the perfect balance—just enough sweetness to temper the bitterness. I wondered if life ever offered that kind of balance too.

We passed around more spoons with increasing concentrations. The final chocolate flight—the 100 percent–was the most bitter.

Bracing my lips and tongue, I wrapped my lips around the tip of the spoon and instantaneously needed water. There was not enough saliva in my mouth to be able to separate my tongue from the roof of my mouth with the layer of chocolate cementing them together. With a swig of water, I was able to dilute out the chocolate and start to clear my mouth of the remaining chocolate.

Gianni, his eyes sparkling as he spoke, started to explain the origin story of hot chocolate. You could see the joy in his eternal smile as he explained how the Mayans had discovered cacao. He was animated, excitement leaping out through his words. You could see how much he loved sharing his passion with others. He had such a gentle way of interacting with us and the world around him, much like the stingless bees he employed to make his honey.

He continued speaking about how the Mayans used crushed cacao with spices to make a hot drink that eventually evolved into what we know today as hot chocolate. Here, they make a Maya hot chocolate, an ode to the ancient drink of the Mayans. They used 100 percent pure chocolate, blending it with black pepper, cayenne pepper and cinnamon, similar to the Mayans. Thankfully, they can make this with the lower concentrated chocolates.

Most of the group ordered the Mayan, adopting the mindset: When in Rome...or Costa Rica. Wanting to try the local delicacy, I ordered the Mayan hot chocolate, but with 67 percent cacao. It was much more subtle and earthier than I was expecting with just a touch of sweetness and deeply rich in flavor.

Gianni came back to the table with a large red oblong pod with black streaks down the sides. Taking a large knife, he cut the pod in half, exposing a long white string of cacao nibs. Nibs are the fleshy fruit surrounding the cacao beans. There were roughly thirty of them inside the pod. He started to cut them off, placing them on a plate to be passed around. He showed us how to suck the fruit from around the bean before spitting it out—inviting us to do the same. The fruit was slimy and had little taste. It took great effort to completely get the fruit off the bean. After a minute, I gave up, spitting the bean out in my hand. This fruit, or cocoa butter, is the fuel source for the cacao seed as it grows. Cocoa butter is cultivated to make chocolate as well.

It was quite remarkable to watch Gianni as he showed us how to harvest the cacao. Knowing how many times he had demonstrated this for people, I wondered how he could continue to do so with such passion and joy.

Watching Gianni move through his day with such delight, I wondered what it might be like to find that kind of contentment in work. Maybe it wasn't the jungle or the chocolate—maybe it was simply the joy of doing something he loved, surrounded by people who were happy just to be there.

I wondered if he had ever had a bad experience with a customer or if he'd ever thought about giving it all up and leaving. While I was sure that the former probably has happened, it would be tough to find a reason why. I was doubtful that he'd ever given a thought to giving up.

Are there certain professions that lend themselves to higher qualities of life for its individuals? Is it possible to be happy and have a quality of life even in the professions that yield lower quality of life scores?

It was easy to imagine giving up everything to move down here and live like Gianni—letting joy be my work. But even in this fantasy, I could feel the tight grip of self-doubt. Would my neurotic personality beat me up and disallow me from sharing the same happiness and joy that Gianni seems to radiate so effortlessly?

How much of our work satisfaction stems from the actual work versus our personality type within that context? Watching Gianni and his employees move about, it was easy to dream about creating a much simpler life here—his delight so contagious.

Just as I was about to take another sip of my drink, Sam stood up, his bald head glistening and drenched in sweat. Crouched over slightly, he quickly moved to the counter asking for the bathroom. He did not look good. A tinge of worry crept in.

Gianni continued talking about how he makes the chocolate bars—taking my mind off Sam. I watched as he used a mortar and pestle to crush the cacao seeds, explaining how to create the chocolate liquid from the crushed seeds. He then took the liquid chocolate and poured it into a form.

I could see Sam walking back to our table, looking even worse. Walking quickly to Galina, he leaned over asking her to take him back home as he was unwell.

Soon, the others were focused on Sam as well. He mentioned having a severe stomach and headache that came on suddenly. Grabbing her keys, she quickly got up as Sam apologized for making her step away.

I sat there in stunned silence. I was worried for him—but also relieved. His presence had become a weight. Part of me hoped this retreat would help him heal too. He felt like a stranger who had walked to our table asking for help—our connection being nothing more than his connection with anyone else here at the table.

The minute they left, it felt as though my lungs could fully expand again. It was as if his presence had sucked all of the air from around me. I felt a pang of guilt but soon relaxed into his absence.

As our tour came to an end, the others asked about walking around some to exercise off the chocolate calories. So, under the heat of the afternoon sun, we walked the opposite direction from where we came.

For the first time in a while, I felt free and relaxed. There was no reminder of who I was back home, of what my marriage wasn't, or even of the burnout from which my body, mind and spirit were still reeling.

We walked without knowing our destination until we came upon a family of coati. A cousin of the raccoon, it was the size of a typical housecat with reddish brown fur and a ringed tail. Two babies crossed the path ahead of us, likely following their mother, as we stopped in silence. Being here in this country amongst the wildlife is one of the greatest gifts I will have ever given myself. The sight of wild creatures moving freely through the forest continued to awaken something youthful in me—a pure and giddy wonder that I had not felt in years.

After they passed, we realized that the gates to the inner sanctum of the park were closed and as the sun was starting its descent, we decided it best to turn around and head home to prepare for tonight's outing.

CHAPTER 34

The Universal Gift of Falling Apart

THE PREVIOUS DAY, WE had discussed going to Santa Teresa to hear Galina, her husband, and her father sing with a friend's band at the opening of a French bistro. Everyone showed interest in going—except for Sam. Still feeling unwell, he decided not to go.

As we drove through Montezuma, the sun had begun its descent. I'd assumed Santa Teresa was only twenty minutes from Cabuya. But after twenty minutes with no town in sight, our driver casually mentioned we were still thirty minutes away.

As we wound around the countryside, navigating steep hills, and dodging parked cars and trucks, my stomach churned with each turn and my head grew light. I had never been prone to car sickness—I could read in the car without issue—but perimenopause had changed that. Now, driving at night on winding roads seemed to trigger nausea. The unease in my stomach was matched by a growing sense of doom and vulnerability.

I rolled down the window, hoping the fresh air would help quell the nausea. But, as we coursed through another little town, the air thickened with the acrid scent of exhaust and rubber tires mingling with the rich smells of food from the local eateries. Despite the overwhelming stench, I leaned my head against the window, desperate for any breath of relief even if the air was far from soothing.

As the minutes dragged on, a sense of mild panic crept in—how much longer could I endure this? Lindsay, sitting next to me, must have sensed my unease. She rummaged through her purse and offered me some mints, their soothing potential clear in her eyes. I gratefully accepted, quickly unwrapping one, and popped it into my mouth. Sucking on the minty sweetness helped, but only momentarily—both the nausea and anxiety returned with a vengeance. The longer we drove, the quicker my breathing became. Now hyperventilating, my body was caught in a frantic loop of panic.

As the trip hit the fifty-minute mark, Wilden, our driver, announced that we were in Santa Teresa. Part of me wanted to feel relief, but I was too deep in my panic to register it. I had passed the point of no return. I knew I would not feel better until I could lie down and sleep this off.

Within a few minutes of entering Santa Teresa, Wilden pulled into a small parking lot in front of the bistro. As I opened the car door and stepped out, dizziness hit me like a wave, and I was not sure I could stay on my feet. Leaning against the car, I felt someone gently support me from behind.

It was Letitia. Her voice, soft and reassuring, immediately put me at ease. She slid her arms under mine, steadying me. The kindness hit me before I could speak. As my strength waned, she whispered that she couldn't hold me any longer. She called to Wilden for help.

I had barely enough energy to speak, "I don't think I can stay. I have to get back." My voice, barely a whisper, betrayed the exhaustion that had taken over.

"It's okay, Wilden can take you back. Let him help you—I'm right here," Letitia's voice was steady, almost maternal. She moved ahead of us to open the passenger side door, then called to her mother, "Mom, if you want to head back home, Wilden is going that way, he can take you too."

Despite my weakness, I couldn't help but marvel at the strange turn of events. Just yesterday, I had met Letitia after overhearing her mother's conversation with fellow passengers on the flight from San Jose to Cobano. Now, here we were—fellow passengers once again, this time on our way back to Cabuya. Letitia's hand still held mine through the open window, her grip steady and reassuring. My breathing, though still faster than normal, had slowed enough that the dizziness started to recede. The air here was fresh, a welcome change from the thick, acrid smells we'd passed earlier.

I tried to whisper my gratitude, the words barely escaping my throat, "Thank you, Letitia. I am so grateful that you're here. I needed this." My voice quivered, a mix of relief and something deeper—maybe the comfort of someone offering nurturing care that seemed foreign to me.

"Baby girl, you're okay. You will be okay. Just breathe and relax. You're doing fine," she cooed, her voice soft and unwavering. "I'm not going anywhere until your breathing is normal."

It felt strange to be comforted this way, to experience such a gentle, motherly care. My own mother had never known how to offer this kind of nurturing. When I expressed worries or fears, they were often dismissed. When I was sick, she performed the necessary tasks—taking my temperature, getting me something to drink—but her actions were mechanical, devoid of the warmth Letitia so naturally offered. I could always tell that this type of caring stressed my mom, but I had believed that she did not have the capability to be a nurturing type of mother. She had never experienced nurturing care from her own mother. I had always yearned for this kind of tender attention, but it felt so foreign to be shown it now—especially by someone who had, until yesterday, been a complete stranger.

This was the kind of care I had never received from my own family. Yet here I was craving it.

In this moment, I couldn't be strong for myself. I knew, deep down, that my body was far beyond the point of handling this on its own. I resisted the urge to push away Letitia's help, aware enough to recognize that if I didn't accept it, I wouldn't be able to stop the panic attack brewing inside me.

I relinquished all control and sank into Letitia's calming words and touch—doing as she instructed. I slowed my inhalations and exhalations, trying to match her calm rhythm. Within minutes, my breathing steadied, and the nausea in my stomach began to ease. For the first time in what felt like hours, I had a flicker of hope that I might make it home without being violently ill—something that felt out of my control just moments ago.

Letitia thanked Wilden for taking me and her mother home, speaking for another minute or so. This allowed me a little more time to steady myself before we started moving again. As the goodbyes faded, Wilden put the car into reverse and slowly backed up to turn around in the parking lot.

I quickly realized that my body hadn't let go of the motion sickness—it retained the memory of each twist and turn. Fresh waves of nausea crashed over me almost immediately, and I found myself desperately focusing on distant points ahead, trying to make sense of the motion my body felt but couldn't reconcile with the stillness my eyes saw.

I had hoped that sitting in the front seat would help quell my motion sickness, but the thick, oppressive blackness of rural Costa

Rica offered little on which to focus. The only light came from the car's headlights, cutting through the darkness in fleeting bursts.

We drove the same winding road we had taken before, but now, as we crested hill after hill, I couldn't see the road beneath us. Each moment felt like a vice tightening around my stomach, each turn more unbearable than the last.

About halfway back, my consciousness began to slip in and out. My eyes would involuntarily shut for a few seconds, only for me to force them open again, each time with more effort as the vertigo intensified. This cycle continued for what felt like an eternity— fifteen minutes that stretched into hours, the world spinning in a blur I couldn't grasp.

During the brief moments of consciousness, I realized with a sinking feeling that I had lost control of my breathing. The steady rhythm I had clung to—counting in for four seconds and out for four seconds—had slipped from my grasp. I had started to hyper- ventilate again, and with it, the fear that my body was betraying me only worsened.

Panic spread throughout my body as I realized that my carbon dioxide levels were plummeting, furthering the sense of losing control. My body's innate response to this was to take my brain offline. When carbon dioxide levels drop too low, the brain shuts down to stop the hyperventilating, giving the body the chance to regain balance.

But this realization didn't bring comfort. Instead, it fueled the terror, making my breathing even more erratic, compounding the nausea that gripped me.

We were the only car on the muddy road, surrounded by pitch-black darkness, broken only by the harsh beam of Wilden's headlights. Waves of dizziness and fear crested, crashing over me with relentless force. Every nerve screamed in protest, and every breath fought against the rising flood of dread. I was trapped in the eye of a violent storm within my body, my world tilting beyond my control.

Suddenly, alarm took over. I grabbed the door handle, blurting out, "I'm going to be sick, I have to get out." I didn't even think—I just flung the door open and threw myself out of the still moving car.

My legs buckled beneath me as I stumbled a few feet into the dirt embankment, collapsing onto my knees and elbows.

The world spun wildly, and I couldn't stop it.

Wilden, startled, stopped the car, rushing out to help me. As I crouched on all fours, my world felt like it was flickering in and out—one moment I was barely conscious, the next I was spiraling back into reality. I tried to force my limbs to hold me up, but they trembled with the weight of fatigue. My body felt too heavy to lift. Too weak to support itself. I could barely keep my eyes open. It was as if every ounce of energy had drained from me, leaving me a shell of exhaustion.

"Please, ma'am, get back in the car," Wilden pleaded, his voice heavy with worry. I could hear the tension in his words, the internal conflict he must have felt—his desire to help, to move quickly, tempered by the knowledge that I could barely stand.

It wasn't just concern—it was the helplessness of someone who couldn't fix what was broken.

"I can't. I can't stand up," my words punctuated by my shallow breathing. I wanted nothing more than to collapse right there on the side of the road, to give in to the exhaustion and let everything slip away. The thought of getting back in the car, of continuing the journey, felt impossible. I wanted him to just leave me, to let me pass out in peace. But even as I thought that I could feel his arm on my back, silently urging me to get back into the car. He would never leave me like this. I could hear Letitia's mother calling out from the backseat, urging Wilden to help me get back into the car. And despite the darkness I felt in my soul, I knew they were right. I couldn't do this alone.

"Fine, but I can't get up by myself. I need help," I finally said, the words tasting foreign on my tongue.

Asking for help had always felt like admitting failure—like confirming every voice that told me I wasn't enough. But more than that, it robbed me of the chance to prove my worthiness. Still, in that moment, I knew I had no other choice.

"I'll help you, but we need to get back into the car," he said, his voice softening with more concern, almost pleading. I could hear the weight of the situation in his words, the understanding that things were more serious than I had let on.

He managed to get me back up and into the car, his grip firm as he steadied me. With both hands, he closed the car door, making sure that it latched completely. As he got in on his side, he locked all the car doors with deliberate care as if securing me in place. We still had fifteen more minutes before reaching Wild Sun. I wasn't sure that I was going to make it. Every second felt like a battle, with the fear creeping in that this might be it—just a tiny thought, but it clung to me like a shadow, whispering that I might not survive tonight. I struggled to push it away, to focus on breathing, but the fear lingered, a quiet companion that refused to leave.

In, one, two, three, four
out, one, two, three, four
in, one, two, three, four
out, one, two, three, four

The momentary pause in motion, as the car slowed, felt like sinking into the earth itself. For a few precious seconds, the dizziness and nausea ebbed, giving me just enough time to regain my bearings. The stillness outside the car was a fleeting treatment, but

I knew it was only temporary—the storm inside me would return as soon as the car started moving again.

When we finally pulled into the entrance of Wild Sun, I felt a wave of relief as I paid Wilden for the fare, my hands trembling slightly as I thanked him for helping me and for taking me home. Part of me wondered how relieved he must be to have me out of his car and out of his care. The thought of being a burden made me uncomfortable, but perhaps, I reasoned, this was his preparation for being a father. I turned and glanced up the incline toward the village of outhouses at the base of Wild Sun. My legs were heavy and unsteady as I took in the road ahead of me. Relief washed over me when I saw Manuel walking just ahead of me.

At least now, I wouldn't have to face the rest of the journey alone.

"Manuel," I called out, my voice faint but clear, "would you be able to help me?" Asking for help had always felt like surrender, like weakness, but at that moment, I knew I could not make it on my own. I knew that I must look like a woman who had too much to drink–stumbling and disoriented. I tried to explain, telling him about the car sickness and panic attack that had drained me so completely. But even as I spoke, I felt a flush of embarrassment—feeling out of control in front of a stranger and asking for help. It made me feel small and helpless.

"I can't make it back to my room by myself. Can you help me walk back there?" not able to contain the desperation in my voice. It was hard to admit that I couldn't do this, that I wasn't strong enough to make it alone. Yet, I was comforted and touched by his apparent concern and willingness to help.

"Of course," he replied sweetly as he offered his left arm to me, allowing me to feel less alone.

"Do you have any Sprite around? My stomach is so queasy still and I need something carbonated to help calm my stomach," I asked.

"I'll go check after I take you back to your room," he responded.

We walked slowly up the main road, crossing the clearing where we eat our meals, the silver moon overhead casting long shadows across the grass. With each step, my anticipation of getting inside to lie down increased as we made it to the deck of the condo. I felt a deep sense of relief wash over me. Soon, I would be able to lie down, close my eyes, and finally let go of the tension that had held me captive for the last two hours.

As I opened the glass sliding door, Sam was sitting up in bed, his voice breaking the silence with a casual question, "You're home early. How was it?" His words felt distant, as though he were asking out of habit rather than genuine concern.

I took three steps in and immediately fell to my knees and slid the rest of my body down onto the cool tile floor. The shock of the sudden release made my breathing slow, but my mind felt heavy, as though it couldn't keep up with what was happening. I could hear Sam scrambling to his feet, rushing to sit beside me, asking question after question, but none of his words registered. My brain was too muddled, too overwhelmed to focus.

There was a knock at the door and Sam stood up to open the door. Manuel had brought a Pepsi and handed it to Sam explaining that he had helped walk me back. He left and Sam returned to the floor, opened the Pepsi bottle, and handed it to me.

"Why don't you just get into bed?" he asked, his voice quiet but unsure. There was an odd hesitation in his words, like he wasn't sure if he should be offering help or simply leaving me to recover on my own. The lack of ease in his suggestion made me realize just how disconnected we had become—how much we still didn't know how to be around each other.

Too exhausted to speak in full sentences, I muttered, "Can't." I tapped my knees and my elbows, the dirt still clinging to my skin–a silent testament to my earlier collapse into the embankment. I was too weak to talk or do anything.

"Well, then go take a shower," he offered.

"Can't. Need help," I muttered, my voice thin and muted, sounding more like a cave woman than the woman I once thought I was. I hated how much I needed help, how helpless I felt. But the truth was, I was too far gone—too worn to pretend I could do it alone anymore.

"Okay, well, sit up and take your dress off and I'll help you," he offered, his voice soft and steady. His willingness to help made my chest tighten. Part of me wanted to resist and pull away, but another part of me recognized that I couldn't, that I needed him in this vulnerable moment. It felt odd, almost intimate, to be cared for this way by someone I had grown so distant from. But in that moment, I didn't have the strength to keep proving anything. I just needed someone to help me stand.

"Need help," I repeated, the words feeling like they were dragging themselves from the deepest part of me. They sounded so weak and raw, but I had no other options.

He gently lifted my upper body off the floor and gently untucked the dress from beneath me, lifting it over my head and helping me to lift my arms up. He got up and helped hoist me off the floor.

Moving towards the bathroom, he went in to turn the water on in the shower, leaving me to strip off the last remnants of clothing. He then motioned for me, a signal that the water was now perfectly warm, and grabbed my arms to steady me.

His touch was both reassuring and a reminder of how distant we'd grown–how much I needed him.

It had been years since my second c-section that he'd had to help me shower. Normally, this would have been a source of deep embarrassment. Our relationship has been so distant, so strained the last few years, that allowing him to care for me in this way would have felt impossible.

But tonight, I had no choice. The pride that normally kept me from accepting his help was buried under the weight of exhaustion and fear. I was forced into this vulnerability, and as much as I hated it, I couldn't fight it.

It took the universe dragging me to the edge of collapse to teach me what I had refused to learn: asking for help was not failure—it was survival.

I stood in quiet acquiescence as he took the loofah and bathed me, gently washing away the dirt that had been ground into my skin at the knees, forearms, and elbows. I pushed away the two sides of the shower walls with my hands to support myself standing until he was finished.

Getting out, he handed me the towel. I dried myself off slowly, each movement heavier than the last. As I finished, I saw that he had already laid out my pajamas on the bed.

His actions were gentle and considerate, but there was a strange tenderness in them that both comforted and unsettled me. He helped dress me, then led me over to the bed, tucking me in.

My body sank into the softness of the mattress, the cool breeze from the air conditioning caressing my skin. Every muscle in my body finally gave way, unwinding in a slow cascade of exhaustion. As my eyes fluttered shut, my brain instantly went offline. There were no more thoughts, no more feelings—just the quiet relief of surrendering to rest.

CHAPTER 35

In the Stillness After the Storm

THAT NEXT MORNING, LIKE clockwork, my eyes flew open around 5:30am. Slowly, the memory of the previous night's events came to the forefront of my mind. I worried about how I would feel getting out of bed.

Unlike having a hangover the morning after a heavy night of drinking, I was relieved to feel that my head was clear and there were no lingering effects from my vehicular vestibular incident and subsequent panic attack. In fact, I felt more energized this morning than any previous morning this week.

As I grabbed my phone and glasses to head out for my daily sunrise meditations, a thought emerged. Perhaps, last night was actually a massive expulsion of all of the negative energy, trauma, pain and outdated and maladaptive narratives disguised as the perfect storm of motion sickness and anxiety. I had asked the universe for help, for direction and guidance.

Was last night part of that plan?

As I sat there basking in the warmth, waiting for the sun to make her entrance, more questions emanated. Slowly, my intuition confirmed what I knew to be true.

Like John Coffey, the fictional gentle giant from *The Green Mile* who absorbed the pain of others, I realized my body had expelled what it could—taking on too much, for too long.

The burden of carrying so much—weighing me down like a suit of armor—was also preventing me from feeling any light, love or joy. I had started to realize that it wasn't that I had stopped being a people person, but rather a barrier had been erected within me, preventing me from connecting with the world around me. I had become untethered from my life, trapped inside my body alone and scared.

This morning, I felt lighter, almost breezy. It was as though huge chunks of that barrier were breaking away and I could really expand back into the world at large. Like coming up from underwater right before you run out of breath and taking that first huge inhalation of air, I had this surge of relief from all that had held me down for so long. I had started to get a sense of what I needed to do to create a more sustainable life for myself.

In thinking of the previous night, I also realized that if it hadn't been for the help of so many strangers, new friends, and Sam, I wouldn't have made it back home safely. I've become more curious about why things unfold the way they do. So when I asked myself why everything happened as it did, the answer became clear: I had become proud of how much I could accomplish on my own—how far I could push myself physically, mentally, and emotionally. But by asking for help, I could no longer cling to those accomplishments. And really—who were they for? I hadn't been seeking praise. I was simply trying to prove I could do it all alone. But last night, I was too weak to keep proving anything. It was a hard lesson to learn, and even in my most vulnerable state, it was incredibly difficult and humbling to ask for help—especially from Sam.

I'm uncertain if it is pride that prevents me as much as it is the fear of feeling shame that inhibits me from asking for and receiving help. In that moment, I felt a surge of gratitude, not unlike what Ebenezer Scrooge felt on Christmas morning after the previous night's yuletide apparitions. It took the weight of the universe to bring me to my literal knees before I learned that *strength is not in bearing it alone, but in reaching out and letting others share the load.* This is difficult to do when one is made to feel like a burden from an early age.

Last night was definitely not a comfortable learning environment. I've come to realize that the life lessons that are learned through hardship are often the ones that create the most resounding change. Much like weightlifting, where muscles grow through regular resistance and time, the brain grows best when it persists through struggle and effort. While I could argue that my life has been a lot of struggle and effort, none of it strong enough to instigate much change. I still could not ask for help. I continued to feel bad about myself should help be thrust upon me. I maintained excessively high, mostly unattainable standards for myself thinking that this was the only way to keep myself from being useless, unworthy and without value.

Up to this point, I had read a lot about psychology, neuroplasticity, burnout, and self-care. But reading about it from the comfort of home hadn't sparked the same kind of change. Last night had. It felt odd to ask for help and it made me feel vulnerable, a sensation with which I thought I felt comfortable. I thought that vulnerability was the ability to share my inner world with strangers without fear.

However, I was beginning to see how I perceived needing help as the ultimate weakness and this was the crux of my vulnerability.

I have long been the one who has had to do and figure out everything by myself. Things had not gone well when asking for help growing up. So I learned quickly to be self-reliant, a characteristic that most likely sent me spiraling downwards into this cataclysmic physical, emotional and mental shut down.

CHAPTER 36

Somatic Wisdom

AS THE SUN ROSE further into the sky, I realized how late it was and quickly readied myself for the last yoga session for the week. As I took my sandals off and walked onto the platform, Sonja and Galina looked up at me.

"I'm surprised to see you, Sarah," Sonja said.

"I actually feel great this morning. Though, I am really worried about this afternoon's activities," I said, saddened by the possibility of missing out on the boat trip to see marine life.

Galina added, "Yeah, that may not be the best idea for you today."

I didn't want to risk spending hours on a boat with no escape from the constant rocking, potentially having another episode of motion sickness. After last night, I didn't want to test my body again.

As we started the final yoga class, I took a deep breath pushing my belly out as far as it could go soaking in all of the glorious jungle air before pausing. Using a lion's breath, we exhaled forcefully, tongues out, mimicking a lion's roar. Said to release tension and toxins, this technique gives confident energy back to the body.

"I can do this," I said to myself silently. "I can implement this practice into my daily life back home."

As I held the poses, I could feel how much stronger I felt today as compared to Monday. I felt more relaxed in my stretches and more energized.

As our practice came to an end and we lay there in savasana pose, Linea played a song she had played earlier in the week. Today, the words had a much deeper impact as the hauntingly beautiful music wove through the air. It begged us to remember why we came here.

For me, this meant letting the lessons be my guide, preventing me from pushing myself back into burnout. These deeply felt revelations had struck me to my core—never to be forgotten. Remembering why I came here became part of my mantra, a gentle reminder of the power in choosing my future.

Coming to this retreat helped my body begin detoxing from the relentless tide of stress hormones. The damage had already been done, but the real work—the sustainable healing—would need to continue back home.

But, the human body is a miraculous thing. In its infinite wisdom, it can heal and repair itself without any input from my mind. I needed to stop living inside my sympathetic nervous system. In doing so, I was continuously bathing my body in those stress hormones.

Not unlike a recovering addict, I needed to be more conscious of my surroundings. Just as a recovering alcoholic is not going to walk into a bar, I needed to create boundaries for myself, bringing more awareness to anything that might trigger me back into fight or flight mode.

CHAPTER 37

Smile Because it Happened

AFTER YOGA, I WALKED back to our condo to get ready for breakfast. Sam was getting out of bed.

"How are you feeling this morning?" he asked.

"Great," I responded feeling relaxed and happy and a little tired. In just five days, I felt stronger, both physically and mentally.

I was proud of the steps I had already taken to get to this point. I smiled as I walked outside, once again dousing myself with enough bug spray to ward off an army of disease-carrying insects.

Sam, Sonja, Galina and I ate breakfast together, while Tammy and Lindsay slept, still tired from the night before. The last day of anything is always sad and breakfast this morning was no different. I had come to realize how much I enjoyed being around these women and how relaxed I could be in their company. We came from all over the world to be here together and when this week was over, we would return once more to our own homes, hundreds if not thousands of miles away from each other. We'd talked about keeping in contact still, if only virtually.

While I was enjoying my morning, melancholy hung over my

head, knowing that we were leaving tomorrow. The line, often attributed to Dr. Seuss, sprang into my mind.

Don't cry because it's over. Smile because it happened.

I still had the rest of today and tomorrow morning before leaving this amazing country. I tried not to think about our departure. For today, I could still smile.

CHAPTER 38

Becoming the Author of My Life

AS THE LAST DAY of our seminar wrapped up, Sonja asked us to bring all that we'd learned together to start creating a more sustainable life.

She asked, "What motivates you, both professionally and personally?"

In recognizing my calling to halt generational trauma, I knew that I wanted to build a home for my children where they could grow up knowing their inherent worth and learn how to create their own emotionally sustainable lives.

Learning the importance of asking myself what makes me happy, I began asking a new question—not what others needed from me, but what I truly wanted for my life. For the first time, I wasn't shaping my life to fit someone else's mold—I was shaping it for me. I deserve to be happy in my own body, living by my own rhythm, creating a life that reflects who I truly am.

For so long, I thought my life was to be given in service of all others, with no regard to my own desires. Without boundaries, I had given up autonomy. No one had taken it from me—I had offered up my own agency.

I'd never asked myself what my ideal life looked like. I could never answer the question, "What will my life look like in five years? Ten years?" I'd assumed that life was what happened to me rather than something that I could direct.

As I started to reflect on how to build a life grounded in my core values—family, empathy, authenticity, spirituality—I realized I had spent the last decade living as if I had no family, placing my identity as a veterinarian above everything else.

Dread had started to take root.

I recognized that this wasn't the first time dread had tried to warn me. A memory surfaced—quiet at first, then vivid.

I had agreed to go speak at a church function as a favor to a client. It was a weekend, time meant for my family. Shame had coerced me into saying yes. That morning, I had been slow to get ready—slow to get out the door. I hated being late. Flustered, I tried carrying too many things in my arms as I got into my work truck. As a result, I dropped both my coffee and my water bottle, watching them quickly roll down the negative-slope driveway and across the street. I groaned loudly with frustration as it built into rage. I slammed down the rest of my bags and ran inside, running up the stairs and back into my bed. Sam followed me up. I told him to call my client and tell her that I was sick. I stayed there in a fetal position until my body calmed.

In retrospect, I had failed to recognize the earliest signs of dread. The full-blown tantrum had been my body's final warning, demanding my attention.

Moving forward, I knew I needed to start paying more attention to how my feelings show up in my body rather than ignoring them.

I chose to let it be my teacher—to show me how to step into the life I was beginning to create. I started to understand that anger and frustration could be messengers—pointing to where my boundaries were being ignored or my goals quietly dismissed. Rather than pushing those emotions away, I began to see them as signals—flags waving me toward what needed care, clarity, or change.

Suddenly, the future—invisible to me before—was starting to become clearer.

As it neared noon, Sonja stopped teaching, thanking us for allowing her to teach us this week. Sadness crept over me as she spoke.

CHAPTER 39

The Clarity Blooming Within

AS GALINA STARTED TALKING about the day's itinerary, I found out that neither Tammy nor Lindsay was going on the boat tour. Sam and I had decided that since we had both felt sick the day before, we were also going to skip the tour. The four of us decided to lunch together one last time.

Sam and I languished on the deck reading while we waited for lunch. I heard the sliding door from next door open as Lindsay stepped outside.

"Hi," I said, "Did you guys have fun last night?"

"Yes, we did. How are you this morning?" she asked with concern.

"Fine. I was not good last night, but this morning was so much better," I answered.

"I'm glad to hear that. You did not look good last night," she said.

Suddenly remembering that I had forgotten to get the name of the song she had mentioned during our first day here, I asked for it again.

"It's Lark Ascending by Vaughan Williams," she told me. Then, she said, "Hold on. What's your phone number? I'll text it to you."

As we talked, the conversation slowly moved from light to meaningful—as they often do when two people feel safe in each other's company. There were things she shared that I'll hold quietly because they're not mine to tell. But in the space between our stories, something opened in me. I found myself sharing something I hadn't expected to say out loud.

"I was married to a narcissist before Sam," I said. As I spoke about the brief, but dysfunctional relationship, Tammy joined us. I continued, "I sat on the therapist's floor as he yelled at me. As I was crying and begging him to stop, he left, slamming the door behind him. Sobbing, I looked to the therapist, asking, 'What can I do to make him love me more?' She paused a second, telling me that she thought he loved me as much as he could."

Tammy abruptly stood up and excused herself, going back into the condo. I could sense it was something I had said that had upset her. I quickly looked at Lindsay with panic in my face automatically apologizing for whatever I had said that might have upset her.

"Stop," Lindsay said as she leapt up to within two feet of my face, "Stop. Don't do that. Do you know what you did?"

Startled by Lindsay's direct and authoritative manner, I frantically searched for the answer. I had no clue. I had merely spread out a blanket apology for whatever I had said that might have triggered Tammy.

"You took responsibility for something that was not yours to take," she said, pausing. "And, she needs to hear this. She needs to hear your story. But, you do not need to take responsibility for her reaction. That's not yours to take."

She then looked at Sam and said, "Did you see that? You should have some sort of word or look that will encourage her to stop assuming guilt in the moment."

I was amazed by how clearly she could see this and touched that she cared enough to say something—not wanting to see me be my own tormentor.

As Sam and I spoke about this later, he said how impressive it was that she was able to recognize that and jolt me into conscious-ness. Much like a near-death experience, where people say their whole lives flash before their eyes, I had the same experience—only mine was emotional. I was watching, in fast-forward, every moment where I had assumed responsibility for the emotions and feelings of others. It was second nature, automatic. But in that moment, something cracked open. It was as if Lindsay's words cut through the static in my brain, and I saw the pattern clearly for the first time.

And just then, as if in response to the clarity blooming inside me, the sun peeked out from behind the clouds.

CHAPTER 40

The Barefooted Exhale

AFTER LUNCH, SAM AND I decided to walk into town and to the beach. I have always loved the ocean and I wanted to spend my last day in this tropical paradise exploring.

With the high humidity, leaving the protective covering of the jungle left us doused in sweat from head to foot. We barely made it twenty yards from the entrance to the rehab facility before we started panting. As we walked leisurely down the mud-packed road towards the little town, I noticed that my shoulders hung low and relaxed. It was an odd, but good feeling. The contrast between that and how I normally held them, clenched up near my ears, was stark. So much had happened this week, but today, the tranquility was palpable—my body finally and completely relaxed. There was no evidence of the anger, stress, fear, and urgency that brought me to Costa Rica.

There was an easiness in Sam's presence as well, a softness that hadn't been there before. He would tell me later that my need for his help the night before had ignited a desire to be more present in our marriage and to be more nurturing towards me.

By the time we reached the main road into Cabuya, our clothes were soaked. I rolled my yoga pants up to my knees without any concern for how I looked. I did not feel any external judgement as we walked. This lack of judgement, so foreign to me, was beguiling. I wished that I could stay and bask in this feeling forever.

We found the tiny little shop, an indication to make a right turn down a mud road that ran straight into the Nicoya Bay.

Anticipation bubbled within me as we got closer, hearing the sound of the water hitting the rocky beach. Ahead of us, a small land mass rose above the waters—Cemetery Island. It was largely uninhabited, except for those buried there. The island had been used since the 1700's by the local indigenous people as a burial site for their loved ones.

Galina told us that twice daily, the rocky sea floor exposes itself allowing people to walk across the parted waters to the island. Unfortunately, we arrived too late or too early to get there.

Instead, we walked parallel to the island along the rock and basalt beach. A committee of black vultures was resting on the basalt as we walked, unfazed by our presence. They were the perfect embodiment of the cycle of life–a symbol of my own cycle, from despair back to living and thriving.

As we walked barefoot and carefully along the rocks, a cheerful stray dog appeared at my side, his tan fur mostly gone—the lichenified pigmented skin exposed. He trotted happily alongside me enjoying our company. He would periodically stop to scratch, jogging back up to us as we continued down the beach.

There were no other humans to speak of besides a couple who sat sunbathing completely nude. Showing no concern for our presence on the beach, I thought about what it would be like to walk around without worrying what others thought.

The sounds of the tiny horseshoe crabs, their tiny claws

scratching against the rock as they crawled, excited me–my child-like awe bubbling to the surface. I had to take a video so that I could capture the sound that thoroughly filled me with wonder.

I looked up, realizing that I had fallen behind Sam quite a bit, and hurried to catch up. Next to where he was standing, there was a large tree trunk that jutted up from the shore, twisting as if a tornado had created the tree trunk and its branches in its image. The branches were truncated. Above it, the clouds had formed a similar twisted and scattered pattern as if the universe had conspired to create a piece of art just for me. I stopped to capture this moment.

CHAPTER 41

Clinging to the Last Light

THE SUN WAS STARTING to fall behind the tall trees that lined the beach and though the temperatures were falling a bit, the afternoon's heat and humidity had left us feeling drained. Knowing that we had a decent hike back up the hillside into the jungle again, we said goodbye to the wild and untamed beauty of the beach and listened as the waves hit the shore one last time before turning to walk back home.

By the time we got back to the condo, Sam and I were saturated with sweat. Our only desire right then—to cool off in the pool that overlooked the jungle. We quickly changed into our swimsuits and emerged into the tepid water.

I still had not been able to capture video of the macaws in flight. Desperate to do so before leaving the next day, I brought my phone to the pool just in case.

Within ten minutes of getting into the pool, we started hearing them. To the southeast of the pool, there was an enormous Guanacaste tree. We saw three macaws fly across the sky to that tree, squawking as they flew. I readied myself to catch more in flight as I had not been quick enough to take video of them.

It was fascinating to watch them call out to the others nearby. Within minutes, we could hear more calling out from other areas of the jungle. Back and forth they would call as if to say, *"Come here to this tree"* with the response, *"No, you all come over here. We don't want to move."*

In the end, it took about thirty minutes for the original three birds to get thirty more scarlet macaws to come rest in the Guanacaste tree. It was an impressive display of behavior. I had finally gotten my video of the macaws in dazzling flight before the pandemonium of scarlet macaws settled to rest together for the night. The macaws gathered for the evening when they were ready, not when I'd planned—just like every insight this week.

The sun set around 5:30pm as it normally does, and someone had turned on the little globe string lights on the canopy giving a soft glow to the pool area.

Sonja came walking back towards the condo and diverted from her path to come talk to us as we lay, elbows and forearms splayed out on the side of the pool. She had gone on the boat tour and reiterated that my decision not to come was smart. She did not get sick but said that it was really rough out on the water today.

As we talked, I realized how much I was going to miss having meals with her, Tammy, and Lindsay. Tonight, it would just be Sam, Sonja and myself for dinner as Tammy and Lindsay had gone back to Montezuma, for the rest of the day and night.

I was glad to have one more dinner here as the food was unexpectedly delicious. I was really hoping to have fish one more time as the fish was caught that morning and burst with flavor, the likes of which I had never before experienced. Others who had been to Costa Rica had told me how much they loved the food, but there really was something inexplicable about how basic dishes could leave you preferring to eat there again over any Michelin star restaurant. I got my wish—fresh fish and rice paired with my favorite juice, star fruit. The flavors were simple, yet they tasted like a celebration. Not just of the food, but of everything I had learned, let go of, and begun to heal. It was the perfect ending to a perfect day.

CHAPTER 42

Bathed in Light, Held in Kinship

THE NEXT MORNING, I had convinced Sam to watch the sunrise with me. I awoke at my normal time but today, I went over to his bed and woke him too. To his credit, I did not have to do much prodding to get him to wake up.

We gathered our phones and I retrieved my journal, spraying ourselves with bug spray one last time before going outside. I turned to sit on my little bench when Sam reminded me of the rooftop balcony. Having forgotten all about this, I kicked myself for not watching the week's sunrises from up there.

We walked up the spiral staircase to the roof. I took my phone out to record the sounds of the howler monkeys and macaws calling out to each other, not wanting to forget their incredible sounds.

Shortly after arriving upstairs, the sun began her show. From here, we watched as the sun put on her grand finale for the week, her fingers of light stretching across the horizon over the endless expanse of the deep blue ocean below. A large Guanacaste tree stood as a solitary silhouette, its branches extending out like an ancient guardian of the shore. It was a breathtaking display as the heat of the sun increased with each new ray. I knew that this sunrise would be a memory that would stay with me until I took my last breath.

Once the sun had fully emerged, Sam and I crept back down the staircase and got ready for breakfast. Galina, Sonja, Lindsay, Tammy, Sam and I sat together one final time for a full breakfast. Tammy and Lindsay both wore the treasures from their day of exploration in Montezuma. Galina had set out a bunch of artisanal soaps made by a local woman for us to choose from as her parting gift to us. Then, Lindsay took a small, wrapped package out and set it in front of me. She told me that it was a gift from Tammy and her, finding it as they shopped in Montezuma the day before.

Touched by the fact that they had thought of me, I unwrapped the delicate package and found a pair of earrings, much like the ones they were wearing themselves. Asymmetric in their appearance, one earring was a multicolored parrot and the other, longer than the first, was a wavy gold band that held a circular piece colored like the parrot. Having noticed their earrings when we first sat down, I felt a pang of regret over not getting to see the artisanal shops in Montezuma. I loved the earrings and quickly put them on—modeling them for everyone at the table.

Their sweet gift was able to quell that nagging voice that tries to convince me that I care more about others than they do for me. I second-guess every situation no matter how well I get along with new people. That voice inside my head begged the question, "Are you sure they actually enjoy being around you?"

Instead, a smile spread across my face as I felt a bond between these brilliant women and me.

CHAPTER 43

The Sweetest Goodbye

WE FINISHED BREAKFAST AND said our goodbyes. Sonja, Sam and I planned to share a cab to the airport. On the way to Cobano, we discovered that we all had a two and a half hour layover in San Jose. So, we planned to meet back up at the airport there to have lunch together.

I had learned so much from Sonja over the course of the week. How I wished I could convey my deep gratitude for rescuing me. She was a wise and compassionate teacher—the perfect role model for my new life.

As we finished our lunch, once more saying goodbye, she left us one final tidbit of knowledge. Taking a small bag out of her shopping sack, she gave each of us a chocolate covered passion fruit ball. She told us to go to the gift shop and get some, mentioning that she brings a few bags home each time she comes down here.

With hugs and promises to talk soon, we said our final goodbyes and Sam and I turned to find the gift shop. There were so many open jars of chocolate covered fruits and nuts. We sampled, then bought, every single variety—enough chocolate to help lift my mood as we boarded the plane headed back to the states.

As the plane ascended above San Jose heading north, I decided to read my book, avoiding the sadness that had started to creep in.

CHAPTER 44

Being Amongst the Swans

ABOUT THIRTY MINUTES INTO the flight, I sensed the dimming of the skies outside my window. The moon, out in the distance, started to glow brighter reflecting the lowering sun. The horizon was beautiful in its pale peach color that faded into a light rose, then violet, before sinking into the pale blueness of the lower sky. I sat mesmerized, unable to stop staring at the stunning vision.

Without my book as an escape, sadness emerged once again. Instead of judging my thoughts and emotions, I let stillness and curiosity take over. What emerged was the story of the ugly duckling. As I thought about the moment when the ugly duckling sees the swans and realizes who he is, it hit me:

I was that ugly duckling.

Never truly ever feeling like I belonged, I had always felt like an oddity. I was seen as too sensitive—too emotional. My taste in music was odd for my age, and I rarely found humor where my friends did. I hated small talk; deeper conversations came more naturally. Large parties were excruciating.

But, during the course of this week, there had been no small talk. Within the first thirty minutes of arrival, our small group had delved deep within ourselves and shared with the group, trusting each other immediately. These people, with the exception of Sam and Jeremy, had all been through four years of veterinary school and had spent twenty plus years in this field. We were all caretakers and nurturers—it felt encoded in our DNA, this instinct to care for one another.

In my own moments of need, the others were always eager to comfort or offer help. How quickly I felt a part of this tribe of women, strong in their power and knowledge as empaths. They were like me in ways I had not experienced before. Normally the caretaker for everyone else, I had never been surrounded by so many other caretakers. For once I felt safe enough to unravel. I couldn't imagine another place in the world where that would have been possible.

At this point, my vision blurred with tears. I started trembling as the realization hit me.

I was homesick.

I was homesick for the place where I had felt safe and surrounded by such beauty. I was homesick for the place where I could finally feel tranquility, comfort and healing. Finally, I was homesick for the other swans—the amazing women I had just left. I was incredibly grateful for the opportunity to live amongst people like me for the past week—feeling truly seen and heard in such a profound way. I had been cared for the way I care for others for the first time ever. Tears flowed in silent streams down both cheeks while I stared out at the sky watching the colors darken.

As the sky deepened to indigo and the stars blinked into view, I found myself thinking not just about the week I was leaving behind, but the life I had been living before it. A life where belonging felt like something I had to earn—where I twisted myself into versions of what I thought others wanted, just to be accepted. I had spent my life trying to fit in, trying to squeeze myself into a tiny box based on others' expectations. But in Costa Rica, I finally stepped out of that box. I was accepted and nurtured for who I truly was.

It's addictive to feel that sense of belonging and connection. Now, I was leaving that all behind. It felt almost cruel to have touched something so bright, only to let it go.

I felt the way I did after reading *Flowers for Algernon* when the effects of the experimental surgery wore off, returning Charlie to his former self. It was heartbreaking to have felt the one thing that you'd never experienced, only to have to go back to your way of living, knowing what it was like for a brief moment in time.

Was it worth it?

Yes.

Sam leaned over, realizing that I was wiping tears away from my face. "What's wrong," he asked.

"I miss them. I miss Costa Rica," I answered. "It's funny, isn't it? I cried coming down here because I was missing the kids so much and seven days later, I'm crying because I don't want to go back home. I miss them," I said, referring to the extraordinary women I left earlier in the day.

Slowly, sadness gave way to gratitude for the incredible gift I'd been given. My therapist would call this positive reframing—the ability to find meaning in pain, to name growth where once there was only grief. I used to think strength meant doing it all alone. Now I know better. I can be strong and still ask for help. I can be whole and still healing. And I can go home carrying all of it—because now, I know how.

CHAPTER 45

Never Forget Why I Came

WAKING UP COLD AND in total darkness the next morning in my own bed was a shock to my system. There were no brightly colored plants and flowers outside my window nor the calls of monkeys and macaws waking me.

I was met with an undercurrent of sadness and longing to be back in Costa Rica, as I rolled over to see my seven-year-old daughter asleep next to me. For that I was grateful. My children had needed me for emotional support while we were gone.

Lying in bed, I needed to quickly put into play a lot of the things I had learned this past week. I realized that I needed to create boundaries for myself and recenter my priorities.

It was Sunday morning, and I was going back to work the next day. However, I was only working one week before taking two more weeks off for the holidays. Though not planned, it was nice to slowly ease back into my life here.

I was incredibly nervous about slipping back into full-blown burnout again.

"Was I strong enough? Would I be able to stand behind my

boundaries? Could I stay present enough to prevent prolonged periods of anxiety?"

So many questions without answers. I had decided that I must treat myself like a recovering addict or alcoholic. I had to be much more conscientious about where I placed my attention and the environments in which I put myself.

Consciousness flows where the mind goes.

Rather than let my mind—a bucking bronco—drag me on another wild ride, I had to learn to lead the horse.

I discovered years ago not to watch the news as it would send me reeling into the abyss of negativity, fear, anger and profound grief. In the same manner, I would need to be much more cognizant of what I read, social media sites I looked at, and conversations I had with clients and friends.

Feeling motivated, I got out of bed and started making a list of all the major lessons I learned this past week.

First, I had to continue working on letting go of beliefs, narratives and emotions that no longer served me. While I had done a lot of this in the jungle, there was still so much more to expunge from within.

Letting go wasn't a one-time act. It would require vigilance, repetition, and grace.

Second, I needed to learn how to ask for help more often—and not just when I am to the point of pure exhaustion. That one felt like a lifelong assignment. I had to unlearn the belief that asking meant failing.

Third, I needed to learn how to accept help, which was an entirely different beast than asking for it. I grew up believing my self-worth was wrapped up in what I did for others rather than something we are each given freely at birth. Thus, accepting help from others negated my ability to earn love and feel worthy or valuable. In fact, it sometimes angered me when people would try to help me—even after I refused—because it felt like they were taking away my ability to feel good about myself.

I hadn't realized, until I went down to Costa Rica, just how tightly I'd tied my worth to usefulness. And how much it hurt to let go of that armor.

The magnitude of what it took for the universe to knock me low enough to accept help—from Letitia, Wilden, Manuel, and then Sam—hit me hard. I physically and mentally could not help myself that night, and if it were not for all of their assistance, I might not have fared as well.

Fourth, I had to create boundaries—to protect me and my family, but also to protect me from myself and my people-pleasing habit that sent me into overwhelm.

Fifth, I needed to stop picking things up that are not mine—like shame, blame, and guilt. I was so used to thinking that everything was my fault, that I automatically assumed guilt, sometimes before anyone else had even tried to blame me. Saying "I'm sorry" was a protective mechanism meant to prevent another person's anger, which often left me hurt. That had ballooned into taking responsibility for other people's emotions, which left me feeling constantly weighed down. This was perhaps the deepest habit to break. But now, at least, I could see it. And I could name it.

The last thing was that I needed to start moving my body again in a healing way. I had already downloaded the down dog yoga app onto my phone before even leaving Costa Rica. So, I started that morning and had set it in my mind that I would do yoga every Wednesday, Saturday and Sunday mornings in order to keep the momentum of what I had started down there. I enjoyed the post-yoga feeling of tired muscles, inner strength and accomplishment. For that time, my mind was completely focused on making my muscles do what they were asked. There was no time for my mind to create false narratives or ruminate on all its worries. The endorphins that I felt afterwards would continue to feed me the rest of the day.

The first day back at work, I was driving my son to school. On the way back home, I was stopped behind a car that had a license plate holder that said Pura Vida. I had never before seen one and certainly not here in Kansas City. Pura Vida was not just a saying, but a way of life in Costa Rica. It refers to enjoying the simplicities of life and basking in a relaxed and positive manner. I smiled at the synchronicity knowing that it was the universe's way of telling me to revel in the Pura Vida way of living now that I was back home.

When I had arrived at my first appointment that morning, I decided that I was going to play Lark Ascending during all of my appointments softly in the background as a way to calm my nervous system down like Lindsay had said. It also served as a reminder to me of all that I had learned in order to implement these lessons into my daily work life. I started playing the song on my phone on a continuous loop and then opened up my computer to find a gorgeous scene on my screensaver. It was a sky view image of a deep green peninsula and the dark blue ocean waters. Curious about where this was, I clicked on the *like it* option on the screen only to find it was from somewhere in Costa Rica. It was as though life was continually reminding me, like an AA sponsor whose presence is there not only to support me but to keep me accountable. The next day, I was talking to a client who, in the course of her story, talked about the ugly duckling. At this point, my mouth fell open. Each day, I was getting so many messages and reminders that it could not be anything but the act of a protective and nurturing universe to create such a gentle environment in which to return to work. I tried to stifle a laugh at this point for fear of the client thinking I was laughing at her. The same protective and nurturing environment that was created by everyone at the retreat was waiting for me back home to allow me to do the hard work to change my life here.

As the weeks turned one into another, I had started to make some big changes regarding my practice, including subscribing to a transcribing service which would cut roughly six hours of work each week in charting time. It would also make taking notes during appointments and phone calls much easier knowing that I could give my full attention to my clients during this time. I also cut my schedule down by one appointment per day to get me home earlier. While I still have some nights where there is additional work to be done once I get home, those days are fewer and farther between now. I could see how I was saying "Yes" to everyone else but my family. My resentment toward work started to surface because I wasn't protecting my time with my family as much as I was protecting my time with my clients.

Any change is hard and fear-inducing, but I had bullied myself into thinking that if I had stood up for what I needed to do for myself, that I would lose clients and eventually my business. However, numerous clients had acted as advocates for me over the years and reiterated to me that any client who does not understand my need to have downtime after hours, or time away on vacation, was not a client worth having. I just could not bring myself to believe this. However, after spending the money and time in Costa Rica, I realized that I cannot afford to not believe this anymore. It suddenly became easier to stand tall and defend myself against critics.

While I can't stand here and say I'm cured—because I'm not, and may never be—I *can* say that I'm far healthier than I was six months ago. I've told my story many times now, and I no longer feel shame in sharing that I was likely living in burnout for almost a decade—three of those years spent in end-stage burnout.

Just three months before the retreat, I was drowning in shame. I remember breaking down in tears as I told a handful of longtime clients what I had been going through. I've come to understand that I have a personality type—and a personal history—that makes me more vulnerable to burnout. My childhood, my work ethic, my genetics, even my career choice all played a part.

But now, I'm armed with tools. I'm stronger, more confident, and more self-aware than I was even a few months ago. Instead of wearing my exhaustion like a badge of honor, I'm learning to listen—to notice the early signs and respond with care.

Someone recently told me I should return to Costa Rica every year, the way you'd take a car in for a tune-up—to keep things running smoothly. Maybe that's true. For now, I do the little things that remind me: I listen to the song Linea played at the end of our yoga classes. I replay her words in my mind. I remember why I went.

And maybe Costa Rica wasn't the end of the story—just the place where I started telling a new one.

I will not go back to end-stage burnout.

I will stand up for myself.

I will remember why I came.

So I don't repeat history.

ACKNOWLEDGEMENTS

I COULD NOT HAVE written this book without the love, patience, and quiet encouragement of so many who stood beside me.

To my family, who gave me the roots to grow and the wings to fly.

To my friends, who held space for my doubts and reminded me who I was when I struggled to remember.

To my beta readers, Sonja, Galina, Carolyne, Mike, and my mother. Your honesty and generosity helped me polish these pages into my beautifully authentic story.

To Clark, my book designer, for putting up with countless questions while you taught me about publishing and for crafting my story into an exquisite book.

To Keith, who took my vision for the front cover and made it come to life.

To Sonja, Galina, Linea, Lindsay and Tammy, whose spirit of healing opened a doorway I didn't know I needed. You were the swans I needed to live among to finally under- stand that I was never the ugly duckling after all.

To Sam, who gave me the courage to step outside my comfort zone and walk the path toward healing, even when I was afraid.

To Matthew, Alexandra, and Scarlett, who taught me that love does not have to be earned and that healing is possible in their laughter, their trust, and their arms.

To every soul who offered me light, love, or a hand to hold along the way:

This book belongs to you, too.

WELLNESS RESOURCES

Retreats:
- Pura Vida Veterinary Wellness Retreats
  https://www.puravidavetwellness.com/

- Wild Sun Rescue Veterinary Retreats
  https://www.wildsunrescue.org/retreats

- House Call Vet Retreat
  https://www.dreveharrison.com/retreat

- Worldwide Vets – Thrive
  https://www.worldwide-vets.org/thrive

- Veterinary Vacation CE
  https://vetvacationce.com/

Coaching and Support:
- Heartstorming Wellness, LLC
  www.sonjaolsondvm.com

- Soul Shine Space for Vets—Dr. Eve Harrison
  https://www.dreveharrison.com/coaching
  https://www.dreveharrison.com/soulshine
  https://www.dreveharrison.com/house-call-vet-academy

- Veterinary Coaches Collective
  https://vetmedcoaches.com/

- Reviving Veterinary Medicine
  https://revivingvetmed.com/

- Veterinary Hope Foundation
  https://veterinaryhope.org/about/

- American Veterinary Medical Association
  https://www.avma.org/resources-tools/wellbeing

- Veterinary Information Network-Vets4Vets program.
  Confidential, peer-to-peer wellness support for the
  veterinary profession (you do not need to subscribe to VIN
  for access)
  https://vinfoundation.org/resources/vets4vets

- Reviving Vet Med
  https://revivingvetmed.com/

Books:
- *Creating Wellbeing and Building Resilience in the Veterinary Profession: A Call to Life*, by Sonja Olson, DVM, C-MMT

- *Mindful Self-Compassion for Burnout*, by Kristin Neff, PhD and Christopher Germer, PhD

- *Burnout: The Secret to Unlocking the Stress Cycle*, by Emily Nagoski, PhD and Amelia Nagoski, DMA

- *Dare to Lead*, by Brene Brown

Yoga:

- Down Dog app – found on the app store and on google play
https://www.downdogapp.com/

Mindful Moment Apps:

- Calm - https://www.calm.com/

- The Happier App - https://thehappierapp.com/

- Aura - https://www.aurahealth.io/aura

- Breathe – on both the App Store and Google Play Store
https://apps.apple.com/us/app/breathe/id1459455352
https://play.google.com/store/apps/details?id=com.havabee.
breathe&hl=en_US&pli=1

ABOUT THE AUTHOR

SARAH BURKINDINE IS A veterinarian, mother, and lifelong caretaker whose healing journey began when she least expected it—on a wellness retreat in Costa Rica—that became a turning point in her life. After years of living in quiet survival mode, Sarah found herself unraveling, only to slowly rediscover a version of herself she had long silenced.

Her career in veterinary medicine gave her a deep sense of purpose but also exposed her to the emotional toll of compassion fatigue, perfectionism, and burnout. This memoir emerged from her desire to remember what changed—and to help others feel less alone in their own unraveling.

Scarlet Macaw Ascending is her first book, but not her last. Sarah continues to explore future writing centered around healing, self-discovery, and the quiet strength that emerges from deep transformation. She is also a passionate advocate for mental health awareness and believes strongly in the power of therapy and emotional care to change lives.

She now lives in Overland Park, Kansas with her husband and three children. She can often be found near animals, under open skies, or speaking gently to herself in the voice she's finally learning to trust.

www.ingramcontent.com/pod-product-compliance
Lightning Source LLC
Chambersburg PA
CBHW021626120626
46545CB00002B/417